S   HAMBHALA POCKET LIBRARY

THE POCKET
SAPPHO

TRANSLATED BY

Willis Barnstone

SHAMBHALA · Boulder · 2019

SHAMBHALA PUBLICATIONS, INC.
2129 13th Street
Boulder, Colorado 80302
www.shambhala.com

This edition omits the "Testimonia and Encomia," "Sources, Notes, and Commentary," and "Index of Poems and Fragments by Number" from *The Complete Poems of Sappho*, which is an abridged edition of *Sweetbitter Love: Poems of Sappho*.

9 8 7 6 5 4 3 2

Printed in the United States of America

Shambhala Publications makes every effort to print on acid-free, recycled paper.
Shambhala Publications is distributed worldwide by
Penguin Random House, Inc., and its subsidiaries.

Library of Congress Cataloging-in-Publication Data
Names: Sappho, author. | Barnstone, Willis, 1927– translator.
Title: The pocket Sappho / translated by Willis Barnstone.
Other titles: Poems. English
Description: Boulder: Shambhala, 2019. | Includes bibliographical references.
Identifiers: LCCN 2019010827 | ISBN 9781611806915 (pbk.: alk. paper)
Subjects: LCSH: Sappho—Translations into English. | Love poetry, Greek—Translations into English.
Classification: LCC PA4408.E5 B34 2019 | DDC 884/.01—DC23
LC record available at https://lccn.loc.gov/2019010827

for Sarah
her eyes
looking

O coronate di viole, divina
Dolce ridente Saffo.

Alceo (N. 620 B.C.E.)
SALVADORE QUASIMODO, *LIRICI GRECI*

O violet-haired, holy,
Honeysmiling Psapfo

Alkaios (B. 620 B.C.E.)

CONTENTS

INTRODUCTION

In Sappho we hear for the first time in the Western world the direct words of an individual woman. It cannot be said that her song has ever been surpassed. In a Greek dialect of the eastern Mediterranean, she became our first Tang dynasty poet, akin to one of those Chinese of the eighth century C.E. whose songs were overheard thought and conversation, in strict form, and who were said to "dance in chains." In her seventh-century B.C.E. Lesbos, Sappho danced in chains, singing of Kritan altars at night and fruit dreaming in a coma, and always in metrical patterns unseen but musically overheard, like her thoughts, passions, and internal dialogues.

Time with its strange appetite has modernized these ancient voices, making the Tang writer Wang Wei and the Aiolic Sappho fashionable and intimate. The East has preserved a ton of the Tang poets, or, as the Chinese would say, "ten thousand" of those golden birds in the Middle Kingdom. Despite early losses due to the fires of the book-burning emperor Qin Shi Huangdi (ruled 221–210 B.C.E.), China thereafter zealously preserved the work of its poets. But Sappho suffered from book-burning religious authorities who left us largely scraps of torn papyrus found in waterless wastes of North Africa. Such maltreatment has especially modernized her into a minimalist poet of a few but important words, connected often more by elliptic conjecture than clear syntax. But what a full living voice comes through those ruins! Every phrase seems to be an autonomous poem, including a fragment of two words describing Eros: *optais amme:* "you burn us."

One day, when the sorrows of war and hatred weary and fade, many diggers will return to the sands of infinite Egypt, to those rich ancient garbage heaps in the Fayum and to the outskirts of Alexandria, where hellenistic grammarians arranged her strophes in the grouped lines still used today. There we will discover many books of Sappho's, as we have found the books of the gnostic Nag Hammadi Library in Egypt and the scriptures of the Dead Sea Scrolls in nearby Syria. And if we do not find more Sappho, what we have left will still be an intelligible constellation of sparkling fragments filling the heavens from the Great Bear down to the Southern Cross.

Europe's first woman poet combined amazing metaphor with candid passion. But being a woman, she wrote from her dubiously privileged position as a minor outsider in a busy male society. Outside the main business of the world—war, politics, remunerative work—Sappho could speak with feeling of her own world: her apprehension of stars and orchards, the troubles and summits of love, the cycles of life and death, and her chats with Afroditi. She wrote, giving the impression of complete involvement, though even in her most intensely self-revealing poems her words have the jarring strength of detachment and accuracy. She wrote as one might speak, if one could speak in ordinary but perfectly cadenced speech. And suddenly we hear her, half-destroyed, revealing:

> I convulse, greener than grass
> and feel my mind slip as I go
>   close to death.

In another poem she is one of the speakers:

> Honestly I wish I were dead.
> When she left me she wept
>
> profusely and told me,
> "Oh how we've suffered in all this.
> Psapfo, I swear I go unwillingly."
>
> And I answered her,
> "Be happy, go and remember me,
> you know how we worshipped you."

At times, as in the interior conversations of the English metaphysical poet George Herbert, we are the poet.

We become Sappho as she is talking with her friend Atthis or, in the famous ode to Afroditi, conversing almost fiercely with her ally the love goddess. In each case she uses the device of speech in poetry to achieve both close intimacy and objectifying distance. We discover a Sappho who is a wholly distinctive personality as opposed to a voice construed by thematic and prosodic convention. Though clearly descending from a tradition of earlier singers, she is never other than herself. Her contemporary could be Constantine Cavafy, for time does not separate their use of conversation and the recollection of past happiness, or the objective and overpowering confessional voice of these two poets of modernity. Line by line, with relentless and sly frankness and outrage, they construct the biography of a voice.

By contrast, Homer, the first man in Western literary history, is but a shadow in his own poetry. By some he is considered to be two Homers, one of the *Iliad* and one of the *Odyssey,* and by others, an editor whose composite voice combines elements of a bardic tradition. Sappho, despite scanty and often mythical biographical tradition, emerges as a realized figure through her poems. Homer was of the epic-heroic tradition, but it took a lyric age to produce the first major woman lyric poet. Or more justly, we can say that Sappho, along with Archilochos, who lived in the early part of the seventh century B.C.E, created the lyric age of antiquity. She talks, laughs, insults, speaks with irony or despair. As Longinos[1] tells us, she knows how to assemble details from true life to give us the lightning force of sublimity. We find such ecstatic transcendence in later poets, notably in the Persian Sufi poets and the English metaphysical poets, and in the mystico-erotic poems of Saint John of the Cross. But Sappho also conveys a different intensity—easy, spare, and piercing—in the meeting of two lovers, as in this very mutilated fragment, "Behind a Laurel Tree":

You lay in wait
behind a laurel tree

and everything
was sweeter

women
wandering

I barely heard
darling soul

such as I now am
you came

beautiful
in your garments

We know Sappho more intimately than any other ancient poet, with the possible exception of Catullus, who was enthralled by Sappho's poetry, imitated and translated her, and addressed his lover and muse in his poems as "Lesbia." She has permitted us to overhear her longing and intelligence, her humor and anger, and her perception of beauty. Her conversations have the naturalness of a storyteller improvising in formal verse.[2] Though her poetry, with the exception of two complete poems,[3] survives only as fragments, her emerging portrait is as precise and profound as a Vermeer or a Goya. Yet that fresh image exists only as these fragments (some substantial), not at all in the unreliable testimonia, all from at least a century after her death.

A few essential facts can be drawn from external sources—where she was born, her approximate lifetime, a possible exile around 600 B.C.E., and that her fame as a lyric poet exceeded all others in Greek and Latin antiquity. As for her looks, character, family history, her profession and lifestyle, the abundant assertions in later writing are contradictory and mythical, and often no more than pleasant aphoristic gossip. Her father's names are multiple; her husband's name, Kerkylas; someone by the name Kleis is probably her daughter or possibly a favorite young friend. But these uncertainties are what we have. Ovid's *Letters of the Heroines,* 15, on Sappho and Phaon, is beautiful and fantastic and has nothing to do with Sappho other than that its tale reveals and celebrates the poet's enduring fame. I regret that I cannot read about the poets from Lesbos as one can about the lives of such extraordinary figures as Plotinos, Plato, and Pindar. But the absence of contemporary information should not trouble. The world's best-known writer, Shakespeare, wrote in a century of extensive documentation, but his portrait derives only from what may be guessed from the poems and plays and a history of the folio editions. Yet Sappho and William Shakespeare do very well, largely concealed from media fact and chronology but resonating in perfect pitch in their verse.

Sappho was born on Lesbos, an island in the Aigaion Sea a few miles off the coast of Asia Minor. Lesbos was then, as it is today, an island of grains, grapes, redolent orchards, and salt flats, spotted with five coastal cities that each commanded its harbor from a rocky acropolis. Greece is a country of light and sea rock—its source of beauty and too little farmland—and shows off its few precious valleys and plains of fertile land, along with its many hills and mountains, which are often terraced for wheat and olive trees up to their steep tops. Lesbos was unusual in having largely tillable terrain, along with its salt flats, dry hills then wooded, and a three-thousand-foot mountain called Olympos, after the traditional abode of the gods in Thessaly. It was known in ancient times for its grains, fruit trees, and, above all, the large valleys of olive groves. In twenty-six hundred years the island has probably changed very little in its village architecture and landscape. As one should know Baeza and Soria to understand Antonio Machado, or Vermont and New Hampshire to know Robert Frost, so there is no better way to know the images of Sappho's poetry than to see today the light, sea, and land of Mytilini, ancient Lesbos.[4]

The biographical tradition of Sappho begins after her death and is a mixture of possible fact, contradiction, malice, and myth. Virtually all the testimonia are found in later grammarians, commentators, and historians such as Strabon, Athinaios, Herodotos, and Suidas (*The Suda Lexicon*). From all this at least some statements of probable truth may be made. Sappho's birthplace in Lesbos was either Eressos or Mytilini; in any case, it was in Mytilini that she spent most of her life. She was born ca. 630 B.C.E. Her name in Attic Greek (the language of Athens and of the bulk of ancient Greek literature) was Sappho (Σαπφώ), by which she is known, but in her native Aiolic she called herself Psapfo (Ψάπφω). She wrote as she spoke, and the speech of Lesbos was Aiolic Greek. In this work I predominantly use *Sappho*, her Attic name, to refer to the poet. In the poems, however, I have preserved her own Aiolic spelling, *Psapfo*.

Her father's name was given as Skamandronymos, but it also appears as Skamandros, Simon, Euminos,

Ierigyios, Etarhos, Ekrytos, Simos, and Kamon. Her mother's name was Kleis. Some suggest—and some deny—that she married a rich merchant from Andros named Kerkylas, who may have been the father of her daughter, Kleis. She had two brothers, perhaps three: Haraxos, Larihos, and possibly the more shadowy Eurygios. Several poems speak disapprovingly of Haraxos, a young man who paid for voyages abroad by trading wine from his estates and who had spent large sums of family money to buy the freedom in Egypt of a courtesan named Doriha. Larihos was a public cupbearer in Mytilini. We know nothing of Eurygios, if indeed he existed. As for Sappho's personal appearance, there were no statues, coins, or vase paintings until long after her death. But she was frequently referred to as the "lovely Sappho," and with the same authority she was described as short, dark, and ugly, "like a nightingale with misshapen wings enfolding a tiny body." These are the words of the scholiast on Lucian's *Portraits.* Yet the same Lucian, referring to her person, calls Sappho "the delicious glory of the Lesbians." In a poem ascribed to Plato from the *Greek Anthology* (or *Palatine Anthology*), she is called the "tenth Muse." What are certainly Plato's words are in the *Phaidros,* in which he has Socrates speak of her as "the beautiful Sappho." In this, Plato was reflecting at least one contemporary belief in her feminine beauty, and in the existing statues and coins the "nightingale with misshapen wings" is depicted with the idealized features and beauty of Afroditi.

The evidence of her activities is no more conclusive. Sappho lived during the reigns of three tyrants in Lesbos: Melanhros, Myrsilos, and Pittakos the Sage. When she was young, it appears that she and her family went, for political reasons while under Myrsilos, to the Lesbian hill city of Pyrrha, and later, about 600 B.C.E., to Syracuse in Sicily, probably in the time of Pittakos. To have left for political reasons implies that her family was important in city affairs. As for her own social position, there is no question that her wealth and class distinction gave her privilege and, largely, immunity from male domination. Her relationship with men was not, at least in the surviving verse, political or societal but was, rather, a question of affection and sexuality. In perhaps her most famous poem, fragment 31, she is pitted as an outsider woman, for the love of another woman, against an impossibly superior competitor, a man who in her eyes seems godlike and completely excludes her from the erotic agon. In this attitude she differs from her aesthetic cousin, the Shulamite of the Song of Songs, who is one of the earliest voices to speak eloquently and powerfully from a woman's vantage point. The Shulamite celebrates erotic love and protests against the night guards of the city who have beaten her, "those guardians of the walls." Sappho is at least free from the bullying of such "night guards," but is nevertheless confined by her sex to a parallel world of aristocratic women.

This should not suggest, however, that Sappho and other women were viewed by men, or viewed themselves, as equals. Although the Greeks did honor nine male poets—Pindar being first among them—we find Aristotle stating superciliously in the *Rhetoric* (1398b): "The Mytilinians honored Sappho although she was a woman." But with all the hits and misses, Sappho is universally honored as the foremost lyric poet of Greek and Roman antiquity.

The women mentioned in Sappho's poems as companions are Anaktoria, Atthis, and Gongyla; she loved them passionately and shared catalogs of happiness with them, which she recalls with pain and pleasure after they have left her. Other friends are Mika and Telesippa and Anagora; she was angry with Gorgo and Andromeda, who had left her to become her rivals. But of the widely held theory of Ulrich von Wilamowitz-Moellendorff and others that her relationship to all these women was that of high priestess in a cult-association (*thiasos*), or in a young lady's academy of manners, the most one can say is that she was probably known as a teacher of young women. As for using her position of teacher at any level (and surely "cult" is a stretch) as a means of explaining away her homoerotic poems, this is unpleasant nonsense and traditional bigotry, and has no basis in the ancient biographical tradition and no support in the existing remains of her poems. Unfortunately, the cover-up theory, born of moral desire to conceal Sappho's gay romances, remained dominant until the mid-twentieth century.[5]

The ancient commentators have also told us that there were really two Sapphos—one a poet and one a prostitute who also wrote poems—or that Sappho herself was a prostitute, and Ovid recounts the legend that she threw herself from the Leukadian Cliff out of love for the ferryman Phaon. It should be remembered when considering these more extravagant tales about Sappho and her family that there were perhaps thirteen plays dealing with Sappho in later Attic comedy, and that by then she had become a stock figure on the Athenian stage. It was on the stage, her modern apologists contend, that the black legend of Sappho originated. The black legend extended to her husband, Kerkylas, whose name only appears in testimonia found in the late Byzantine *Suda*. The same wild Aristophanic imagination and comic nastiness that portrayed Socrates as a fool standing on clouds and made Sappho into a babbling stage clown surely took shots at her husband, Kerkylas.

As we are told, Sappho's husband was from the island of Andros, meaning "man." In "Kerkylas" one can hear the word *kerkís,* meaning "rod," "peg," or "weaver's spindle," which has led some scholars to speculate that both Sappho's husband's name and his origin were an invention and "indecent pun" from one of the many later comedies—such as the six comedies entitled *Sappho*, the five entitled *The Leucadian*, or two entitled *Phaon*—all lost plays known to us only by their titles, but in which Sappho was a target for lampoon. So, according to ancient comedic reasoning, "Kerkylas of Andros" yielded "Penis of Man," or, in more futsy academic jargon, "Prick from the Isle of Man."[6]

Sappho is credited with certain technical innovations. She is said to have been the first to use the *pectis* (a kind of harp), and to have invented the Mixolydian mode and the Sapphic stanza, which was imitated by Horace and Catullus. Sappho was not the first Lesbian to contribute innovations to Greek poetry. Before her were the semilegendary poets Arion, inventor of the dithyramb, and Leshes, author of the *Little Iliad*, and then Terpandros, who invented and wrote poetry for the seven-string lyre, of whom we have four small and doubtful fragments, the earliest examples of lyric poetry in Greece. Sappho's Lesbian contemporary Alkaios wrote in Alcaics (quatrains in tetrameters), which were also imitated by Horace and other Latin poets.

There is good reason to believe that Sappho was a prolific writer. We do not know how she recorded her work—whether on papyrus, on wooden tablets overlaid with wax, or orally through song—but centuries later, when the Alexandrian grammarians arranged her work according to meter into nine books, the first book

contained 1,320 lines (330 four-line stanzas in sapphics—
three eleven-syllable lines followed by a five-syllable
line; in reality, Sappho used many metric forms, not
only the prosodic form that carries her name).[7] Judging
from this, we may suppose that the nine books con-
tained a very extensive opus. Her work was well known
and well preserved in antiquity. We have Athinaios's
claim in the third century c.e. that he knew all of Sap-
pho's lyrics by heart. But the best indication, perhaps,
of the general availability of her works in the classical
age lies in the number of quotations from her poems
by grammarians, even late into Roman times, which
suggests that both commentator and reader had ready
access to the corpus of the work being quoted.

Of the more than five hundred poems by Sappho,
we have today about two thousand lines that fit into
intelligible fragments, and these come from no sin-
gle collected copy but are pieced together from many
sources: from the scholia of ancient grammarians to the
mummy wrappings in Egyptian tombs. Plato's entire
work has survived virtually intact, having been both
popular with and approved by pagans and Christians
alike. Sappho's work did not lack popularity. As Ovid
put it, "What did Sappho of Lesbos teach but how to
love women?" (*Lesbia quid docuit Sappho nisi amare puel-
las?*) But nonetheless, she did not always win approval.

To the church mind, Sappho represented the cul-
mination of moral laxity, and her work was treated

with extreme disapproval. About 380 C.E., Saint Gregory of Nazianzos, bishop of Constantinople, ordered the burning of Sappho's writings wherever found. She had already been violently attacked as early as 180 C.E. by the Assyrian ascetic Tatian: "Sappho was a whorish woman, love-crazy, who sang about her own licentiousness."[8]

Then in 391 a mob of Christian zealots partially destroyed Ptolemy Soter's classical library in Alexandria. The often repeated story of the final destruction of this famous library by the Arab general 'Amr ibn al-'Āṣ and Caliph 'Umar I is now rejected by historians. Again we hear that in 1073 Sappho's writings were publicly burned in Rome and Constantinople by order of Pope Gregory VII. Until late in the eleventh century, however, quotations from Sappho still appeared in the works of grammarians, suggesting that copies of her poems were still preserved. We will never know how many poems by Sappho were destroyed in April 1204 during the terrible pillage of Constantinople by the Venetian knights of the Fourth Crusade, or by the Ottoman Turks at the fall of Byzantium in 1453.

But apart from official hostility, Sappho's works suffered equally from the general decline of learning in the early Middle Ages and the consequent anger of oxidizing time upon neglected manuscripts. It is probable that some of her work was lost in about the ninth century when classical texts, preserved in uncial script, were selected and recopied in modern letters. No single collection of her poems, in whole or in part, survived the medieval period. Nevertheless, in the Renaissance, Sappho came back into light. Italian scholars found the essays *On the Sublime* by Longinos and *On Literary Composition* by Dionysios of Halikarnassos, which contain two of Sappho's most important poems: fragment 31, "Seizure," and the complete ode to Afroditi (fragment 1, "Prayer to Afroditi"). Every stanza, line, and isolated word by Sappho that appeared in the works of other Greek and Latin writers was assembled, including indirect poems, that is, summaries or retellings of her poems.[9]

Very few fragments of original papyrus manuscripts have survived in continental Greece,[10] but in parts of rainless Egypt in the Fayum, an oasis semidetached from the Nile Valley near Krokodilopolis, important papyrus manuscripts with poems by Sappho were discovered in 1879. The Egyptian expeditions by the English scholars B. P. Grenfell and A. S. Hunt, beginning in 1897, yielded a wealth of material. In addition to important poems by Sappho, parts of four plays of Menandros were found in a refuse heap near Afroditopolis; at Oxyrhynhos, Alkman's maiden-song choral ode, the first in Greek literature, and twenty odes by Bacchylides were discovered. Bacchylides ceased to be simply a name and became again a major poet of antiquity, rivaling Pindar.

But above all, the range of Sappho's work was dramatically expanded. The precious papyri had been used as papier-mâché in mummy wrappings. Unfortunately, many were torn in vertical strips, and as a result the Sappho fragments are mutilated at the beginning or end of lines, if not in the middle. The mummy makers of Egypt transformed much of Sappho into columns of words, syllables, or single letters, and so made her poems look, at least typographically, like Apollinaire's or e. e. cummings's shaped poems.

The miserable state of many of the texts has produced surprising qualities. So many words and phrases are elliptically connected in montage structure that chance destruction has delivered us pieces of strophes that breathe experimental verse. Her time-scissored work is not quite language poetry, but a more joyful cousin of the eternal avant-garde, which is always and never new. So Sappho is ancient and, for a hundred reasons, modern.

Ezra Pound goes back full circle when he "antiques" the form of a poem in order to make it resemble a vertical strip of a Sappho papyrus. His brief poem "Papyrus," addressed to Gongyla, reads:

Spring . . .
Too long . . .
Gongula . . .

But Sappho aces him with an impeccable strip in which plenitude resides in the ruins of her script:

RETURN, GONGYLA

A deed
your lovely face

if not, winter
and no pain

I bid you, Abanthis,
take up the lyre
and sing of Gongyla as again desire
floats around you

the beautiful. When you saw her dress
it excited you. I'm happy.
The Kypros-born once
blamed me

for praying
this word:
I want

In her minimalist Imagist period, H.D., and her descendants in the Black Mountains, learned from Sappho, copied her absences, and found themselves through her losses. William Carlos Williams translated her and Robert Creeley and the Brazilian concrete poets were her immediate kin. But despite this *parenté d'esprit* that truly helped generate our modernist movements, the price of the unwitting modernization of Sappho scripture, through the random damage of her poems, has resulted in the tantalizing loss of intelligibility of hundreds of her fragments, not to mention the disappearance of most of her work.

The cost was also high to the English and German scholars who undertook the labor of unraveling the damaged papyri (both literally and figuratively). The German scholar Friedrich Blass, who first deciphered important poems by Sappho in these Fayum manuscripts, lost the use of his eyes, and Bernard P. Grenfell, the explorer and pioneer editor of *Oxyrhynchus Papyri*, during his intense labors for a while lost his mind. Most hurtful to Sappho were the majority of her defenders from the seventeenth to the early twentieth century, who in their eagerness to clean up Sappho's act, to create a morally sound "divine Sappho," quite lost their perspective of the poet and hopelessly muddled the poet's life with the poems.

While a thousand years of bigotry destroyed the greater part of Sappho's poetry, the zeal of her later defenders, from Anne Lefebvre Dacier in 1682 to Ulrich von Wilamowitz-Moellendorff, Bruno Snell, and C. M. Bowra,[11] to rehabilitate her moral character has not helped the poet's cause, nor has it contributed to our understanding of her work. It is no less than astonishing how otherwise temperate scholars became outraged and imaginatively unobjective at the slightest suggestions by others of moral frivolity on Sappho's part. Not Sappho's poems but Middle and New Comedy and Horace and Ovid are accused of instigating the black legend. Several arguments are offered and reiterated to justify her love poems to other women. The dominating cure was the *thiasos* remedy: since Sappho was a priestess and the head of a circle of young women, these poems did not mean literally what they say; her love poems to women were epithalamia written for ceremonial purposes; the poems castigating her brother Haraxos for his affair with Doriha prove her own high virtue; Alkaios once addressed her as *agya* (holy or chaste); she came from a noble and highly respectable Lesbian family. The arguments read like a brief—in an unnecessary trial.

In the nineteenth century the denial of Sappho's homosexuality prevailed. There were exceptions to an illusory interpretation of her poems, but these were not apparently heeded. We find some notable exceptions in England and a tragic one in the instance of Charles Baudelaire, who paid bitterly for his candor. Perhaps the clearest statement regarding Sappho's sexuality appears in William Mure of Caldwell's *A Critical History of the Language and Literature of Antient Greece*. While the Scottish classicist condemns Sappho for her "scandalous history" and her "taste for impure intercourse, which forms so foul a blot on the Greek national character," he pooh-poohs the standard notion of Sappho's higher "purity" and insists that her Lesbian female "association" was nothing less than the "pursuit of love and pleasure." He writes, commenting sharply on fragment 31:

> In several places, Sappho addresses certain of her female associates in terms of no less voluptuous passion than those employed towards her male objects of adoration. In one passage, equal in power and nearly equal in length to the ode to Venus already cited, her ardour is inflamed by the sight of a rival, a male rival it may be remarked, participating, however slightly, in the privileges to which she herself claimed an exclusive right. She describes it as "a bliss equal to that of the gods to sit by the music of her voice, and gaze on her fascinating smile." At the same time, in anger against her male rival she feels "mortification and jealousy."[12]

In his modern "right on" commentary, William Mure notes, "If Sappho did *not* mean or feel what she has expressed in the passage above, then the most brilliant extant specimens of her muse become comparatively unmeaning rhapsodies; if she *did* so feel, her sentiments were not those of maternal tenderness or sisterly friendship."

A generation later, John Addington Symonds (who had "shocked" Walt Whitman in a letter sent to the American poet, assuming their common passion for men) speaks of Sappho's homoeroticism. He slightly tempers his view of Sappho as a practicing homosexual by contrasting her "sating of the senses" with the cruder voluptuousness of Persian or Arabic art. He writes, "All is so rhythmically and sublimely ordered in the poems of Sappho that supreme art lends solemnity and grandeur to the expression of unmitigated passion."[13] He then laments the ruin of her literary remains: "The world has suffered no greater literary loss than the loss of Sappho's poems."

In mid- and late-nineteenth-century France, official morality and hypocrisy reigned with respect to Sappho's lesbianism. While by the end of the century, there was a fad and rash of lesbian novels and memoirs published under the guise of being "newly found novels by the poetess Sappho," when Charles Baudelaire published his *Les Fleurs du mal* in 1857, *Le Figaro* condemned the book as "the putrescence of the human heart." In large part because of his inclusion of six poems concerning Sappho and *les femmes damnées*, the author and his publisher Auguste Poulet-Malassis were dragged to court, convicted, and heavily fined. The six "lesbian" poems were banned from the book, and Poulet-Malassis was sent to prison. An appeal to the empress Eugénie resulted in the reduction of Baudelaire's fines.

Only in 1949 was the ban on the immoral poems officially lifted.

It is extraordinary that until the mid-twentieth century the myth of Sappho's chaste love remained standard fare. In this cover-up there is an exact parallel with the confused and disturbed denunciations of those who dared to suggest that William Shakespeare was stained by the abnormal emotions of Greek love. Such folly was expressed only by weak critics blind to the poet's metaphysical message and spiritual convention. Oscar Wilde was an obvious exception. He loved the *Sonnets*, he tells us in letters, and he theorized that the young man who received Shakespeare's relentless ardor was actually "a wonderful lad" named Willie Hews, "a boy actor in his plays." On the third and last day of his famous trial of "gross indecency" for a homosexual act in 1895, Wilde invoked the *Sonnets* in his defense, a declaration that served to deepen his legal guilt.

In *Shakespeare's Sonnets*, the editor, Katherine Duncan-Jones, addresses the almost universal dissemblance of Shakespeare's homosexual passions. Without sympathy she describes W. H. Auden's complex manner of reading *Sonnets,* saying that interpretation becomes "entwined with the personality (and sexuality) of the critic, as well as his or her cultural location." She writes:

This is the case of W. H. Auden. Though anyone with a knowledge of Auden's biography might expect him to celebrate and endorse the homoerotic character of 1–126, he was absolutely determined not to do so, at least publicly. In his 1964 Signet edition Auden claimed—as G. Wilson Knight had done— that the primary experience explored in *Sonnets* was "mystical," and he was extremely scathing about putative readers of homosexual inclinations who might be "determined to secure our Top-Bard as a patron saint of the Homointern." Yet his public adoption of this position seems to have been a characteristic instance of Auden's cowardice, for later in 1964 he confessed to friends that a public account of Shakespeare (evidently equated by Auden with the speaker in *Sonnets*) as homosexual "won't do just yet." Perhaps Auden was referring to the changes in legislation then under discussion: Parliament finally decriminalized homosexual acts between consenting adults in July 1967.[14]

By contrast with Auden's prudence, the Alexandrian poet Constantine Cavafy (1863–1933) in the early 1900s fully presented his homosexuality in his poems, which, however, he printed only privately, to give to friends. Despite candor in verse, he too faced the reality of the impossible public plight of gays. Though he was in his lifetime known as the foremost poet in the

Greek language and T. S. Eliot published his poems in 1924 in his *The Criterion*, Cavafy could not permit a collection of his own poems, carefully ordered by his own hand, to be published while he was alive. We hear his own moving statement about public acknowledgment in his prescient "Hidden Things":

From all I did and all I said
let them not try to find out who I was.
An obstacle stood before me and transformed
my acts and my way of life.
An obstacle stood before me and stopped me
so often from what I was going to say.
My most unnoticed acts
and my most veiled writings—
only from these will they know me.
But maybe it's not worth it to devote
so much care and effort to knowing me.
Later—in a more perfect society—
someone made like me
will certainly appear and act freely.[15] [1908]

In England and America Sir Denys Page was the first major academic scholar to oppose all this posturing about Sappho's sexuality. Page, who with Edgar Lobel has produced the most authoritative edition of Sappho's works, chose to look at the texts and found that the poems gave no support whatsoever to the arguments. Page contends that Sappho was not a high priestess; only a small portion of her poems might be considered epithalamia; and Sappho herself, far from being a woman of unfailingly noble sentiments, was a common mortal concerned with common matters of love and jealousy. In deflating the contentions of her supporters, Page also deflates Sappho herself—not without a note of moral reproach.

I have spent some time reviewing the history of Sappho's usually violent encounter with the world, not because one must necessarily know something or anything about an author to appreciate the work, but because in Sappho's case the world has known—or assumed—too much, and this knowledge interferes with any fair appraisal of her poems. The question has been whether Sappho was indeed a lesbian in the sexual—and not just the geographical—sense of the word.

First, it should be stated that whatever Sappho was in her life has very little to do with the content of her poetry; whether she was indeed bisexual or merely ascetic like her contemporaries Jeremiah and Gautama Siddhartha will not change the meaning of her poems. It is not that an author's intention must be discounted, nor need we puristically fear the heresy of intentional fallacy or other critical sins, old and new, including historiological snooping into her time and culture. Yet if the author's intention is meaningful, it must be seen through the text, through the lyrical speaker in the poem, and not merely from outside sources. In Sappho's case the problem is more rudimentary. Even if we could accept outside sources, there is, in fact, no reliable authority outside the poems themselves to explain the author's intended meaning in her many poems dealing with love.

Nonetheless, the preponderance of recent literary research assumes an authoritative understanding of her culture and historical times, which runs the same risks of blunder and uncertainty as in the work of earlier literary critics, including my old heroes C. M. Bowra and Denys Page. How helpful is the work of social historians in reading the poems of Sappho? As ever, there is much to be learned from serious investigation and much to be questioned. And new generations will question again. In these domains none of us is sinless, but as an amateur reader, I prefer the less serious approach that sees Sappho mainly through her work, and reads her work not as document but as art.

To find Sappho, then, the Sappho of the poems, we may look long at the poems themselves. One fragment is addressed to her daughter, Kleis. A few of them may have been addressed to men. The majority are love poems to women. They are passionate poems, self-critical, self-revealing, detached, and intense. If we are to believe what they say, we will conclude that the speaker in the poems experienced a physical passion for her beloved, with all the sexual implications that similar poems between men and women normally imply. (Much of the world's love poetry is homoerotic, and in ancient Greek poetry, the majority of love poems by known male poets, from Ibykos to Pindar, are addressed to other men.) To give the poems meanings that the texts do not support, for whatever moral motive, is to dilute Sappho's language and to weaken and falsify her work. Even though the remains of her oeuvre are scant, the poems should be allowed a plain reading of unimaginative literalness. "Uninterpreted" they speak for Sappho more directly and eloquently than the countertexts of her old defenders.

In the fragments we have left, only a few lines give details of physical love: "May you sleep / on your tender girlfriend's breast." Many speak of her passions. Sappho's best-known love poem, "Seizure" (fragment 31), is an example of her precision, objectivity, and cumulative power. The poem is direct, self-revealing, yet detached and calmly accurate at the moment of highest fever. She begins with a statement of her pain at the sight of the man sitting near the woman she loves, who, because of his envied position, appears godlike to her; she recounts the physical symptoms of her passion for the woman; and with full intensity but without exaggeration, she uses the metaphor of green turning greener than grass to show her suffering, verging on death, because of a love not returned.

Seizure

To me he seems equal to gods,
the man who sits facing you
and hears you near as you speak
    softly and laugh

in a sweet echo that jolts
the heart in my ribs. Now
when I look at you a moment
    my voice is empty

and can say nothing as my tongue
cracks and slender fire races
under my skin. My eyes are dead
    to light, my ears

pound, and sweat pours over me.
I convulse, greener than grass
and feel my mind slip as I go
    close to death.

Yet I must suffer all, even poor

    The poem states a love relationship, but more, it
states the poet's agony when, consumed by love, she
is unable to compete with the rival—a man, a species

with powers inaccessible to her as a woman, and who therefore appears equal to a god. She cannot reach the woman she loves. The woman affects her with paralyzing force, and she can in no way escape, except through words, from the solitude in which she is suddenly enclosed. Her senses are agitated and fail her. She can no longer see, speak, or hear.

As her bodily functions weaken, she moves close to death, her analogue of the *via negativa*. The mystics would describe this state as dying away from space and time. In Daoist terminology, she is moving to the open country of emptiness. There, as in Saint John of the Cross's dark sensory night of aridities, she reaches momentary detachment from bodily senses, which permits her to speak objectively of the symptoms of her passion. She too is "dying from love." And like those who have had intense physical pain, at a certain threshold she becomes a distant observer of herself. Unlike Saint John, however, the night of purgation is not, at least in this fragment, the moment before the joyful night (*la noche dichosa*) of illumination and union.

Sappho's desire is conveyed as a loss of self. She is exiled, as it were, from her desire and remains in a darkness before death. In Saint John this darkness is described as "withdrawal ecstasy." In Sappho the movement from the self into an extraordinary condition of void and separation results in a violent failure of the senses, a seizure, the ekstasis of negative ecstasy (of being elsewhere, but in the wrong place). For the mystics, the second stage is illumination, the discovery of a new self. However, in Sappho this second stage is blackness, the discovery of the loss of self. The catalog of symptoms of her seizure is a universal condition that finds expression in varying diction and metaphors, secular or religious, from Saint Teresa's interior castles and Andrew Marvell's entrapment in the garden to Marghanita Laski's medical analyses[16] and Jorge Guillén's passionate merging in the circle of light. Hers, however, is love's lightless inferno, without union and without the peace that follows union.

Unable to reach the object of her love, there is no fulfillment and no release except in the objectification of her passion in the poem. Yet in her poetry she does indeed reach the world, if not her beloved. Her words, used masterfully, make the reader one with the poet, to share her vision of herself. There is no veil between poet and reader. Here, as elsewhere in her art, Sappho makes the lyric poem a refined and precise instrument for revealing her intensely personal experience. As always, through the poems alone, we construct the true biography of voice. As mentioned earlier, in one poem in the *Greek Anthology,* Plato speaks of Sappho as the "tenth Muse." The ascription of the epigram to Plato, as of all thirty-seven poems ascribed to him, is shaky. What is certain is that these words reflect ancient opinion. Sappho's own expression of the continuity of her words appears in an astonishing line that neither contains silly phrases "worthy of a Muse" nor betrays any of the ambitious glitter and bay leaves in Petrarch's notion of fame. Rather, the intimate voice, serenely ascertaining its future, is prophetic:

Someone, I tell you, in another time,
will remember us.

Sappho is remembered despite the multiple violations of time. The fragments of her poems contain the first Western examples of ecstasy, including the sublime, which the first-century Longinos recognized and preserved for us. They also include varieties of ekstasis briefly alluded to in these pages: the bliss of Edenic companionship, dancing under the moon, breakfasts in the grass; the whirlwind blast of love; the desolation and rage of betrayal; the seizure and paralysis before impossible love; and as all her ordinary senses fail, the movement near death—the ultimate negative ecstasy. Yet even when she has lost herself, her senses, her impossible love, Sappho is remembered. The diversity and clarity of her voice, the absolute candor, the amazing fresh authority of the poetry, whether in addressing a goddess, a Homeric marriage couple, the moon and stars, a sweet apple or mountain hyacinth, a lamb or cricket, a lover or companion, those qualities compelled in antiquity as they do today.

Ordering of the Texts with Respect to Chronology and Other Editions

The order of Sappho's poems in standard editions does not reflect chronology of composition or the author's age. It may, as in the work by Edgar Lobel and Denys Page, attempt to reflect Sappho's nine "books" or, given the losses, the remnants of her collections. Lobel and Page fragments 1 to 117 are presented as clearly by Sappho, and fragments 118 to 213 (none of the longer poems) follow under the title *Incerti libri,* meaning that they are of uncertain ascription. The actual order or grouping within the books is mostly unknown, since Sappho's hand is not there. They were accomplished in hellenistic times. This traditional presentation is thought to have been determined three centuries after Sappho by the Alexandrian scholars Aristophanes of Byzantium and Aristarchos of Samathrace, when her work was alive and well received.

In this edition the fragments have been ordered independently of their traditional numbering, under a logic that is a mixture of theme and implied chronology and event. Here, the poem number generally follows the number established in *Poetarum Lesbiorum Fragmenta,* edited by Lobel and Page, and the Loeb Classical Library *Sappho and Alcaeus,* edited and translated by David A. Campbell. The latter normally has the same numbering as Lobel and Page, though the Greek texts differ. So in most cases, the numbering standing alone refers to the Lobel and Page Greek text.

My reading of letters and words tends to be closer to the more recent editions by Eva-Maria Voigt, Max Treu, and Campbell than to Lobel and Page. Where the poems do not follow the numbering of Lobel and Page, I usually follow Campbell.[17] When Campbell ascribes a poem to Sappho that Lobel and Page ascribe to Alkaios, I also follow Campbell, who always notes the Lobel and Page ascription. I have also consulted the Denys Page transcriptions in *Sappho and Alcaeus*. When one of Sappho's fragments is not in Lobel and Page but is found in Campbell, Ernest Diehl (*Anthologia Lyrica Graeca,* vol. 1), Voigt (*Sappho et Alcaeus*), or Treu, who adds his own material to earlier Diehl, these differences in judgment are indicated. The judgments refer to texts of uncertain ascription—whether to Sappho, Alkaios, or to a late false attribution—and are indicated by "incert."

With respect to Campbell's English renderings, I have found his strictly prose versions excellent and a benefit to all readers. I would use the word "interpretation" to describe them, because the Greek is so uncertain. He has also chosen, with exceptions, to reproduce those lines of Greek that lend themselves to intelligible translation and then his guesses in reading uncertain letters and words are chaste and selective.

Even as a gloss and dictionary they are invaluable, and more so than the existing beautiful poetic versions.

The measure for determining which of the diverse texts I draw from for each fragment has been their intelligibility for translation purposes. At times the Greek is unintelligible, which means that in a number of poems many lines are omitted (Campbell generally follows this practice).

Greek Words in English

The transliteration of proper nouns and common nouns from one language to another is universally transitional and vexing. One cannot be entirely consistent without being silly and awkward. Who is happy when the English render Livorno, Amedeo Modigliani's birthplace, as Leghorn? However, there is radical change. In transliterating Chinese into English, in a generation we have gone from standard English Wade-Giles to standard Pinyin. At the beginning Pinyin was shocking and difficult. Now Pinyin is de rigueur for scholarship, dictionaries, and newspapers, though it remains a difficult replacement. Some frequently used words in common speech have quickly yielded to Pinyin, such as *Peking*, now rendered as *Beijing*.[18] *Canton* (*Kwangchow* in Wade-Giles) is on the way to becoming *Guangzhou*, but that change is challenging.

Rendering the Greek alphabet in English is more challenging because there are so many interests that have imposed their spelling on Greek as it has slipped into other languages. Latin Rome conquered Greece and translated Greek gods into Roman ones. Artemis became Diana, Zeus yielded to Jupiter or Jove. Greek words were transliterated into Latin letters, not always close in sound or feeling. English and the Romance languages have followed the practice of Latinizing Greek names while Germany and Eastern Europe keep closer to the Greek.

While the ancient Alexandrian scholars preserved and fashioned Sappho, ordering and editing her poetry, since Horace and Quintilian there has been war between "grammarians" and "libertines" over the nature of translation itself, between *fidus interpres,* which the Latin writers mocked, and literary re-creation and imitation. In modern times the soft war goes on between translation as a literary art or a classroom language test, which is revealed in spelling. The combatants regularly have seats in the academy, and victory depends on which audience and publisher receives and acclaims them. As for the gods and their IDs, outside Romance tongues the Greek gods have regained their identity. As for the transcription of names, unlike Chinese where one power has enforced its system (notwithstanding holdouts in Taiwan and Singapore), there is no single rule book for regulating transliteration. This free-for-all mode reflects language flux, which is always with us, no matter who is emperor.

With no absolutes on the horizon, what is happening now? Despite the minor brawls, much happened in the twentieth century to return us to equivalents resembling the Greek scripture (though James Joyce did not get the word when he dropped the bomb of *Ulysses*). My own perplexities on the *how* (and here the quandary is not art versus gloss but simply on how to record the change of signs between tongues) at least is typical, and in my weathercock self I spin with each puff of revelation. I have been tinkering with classical Greek for many decades along with Koine Greek and biblical Hebrew. When I undertook the translation of the New Testament, a book from Asia Minor, I chose to restore, as far as one can know, the original Hebrew, Aramaic, and Greek names so that a reader might observe that most of the figures in the scriptures, including gods and demons, are Semitic, not European. So it is Yeshua the Mashiah, not Jesus the Christ. One may recognize that Saint James is not from London or China but a Jew from Jerusalem, and that it would be best to call him Yakobos as in biblical Greek, or better, Yaakov, reflecting his name in Aramaic and Hebrew. Similar convictions about reflecting original language and place have led me to a spelling I have presented, with variations, in rendering Greek lyric poetry and the philosophers Herakleitos and Plotinos.

The main lesson from all this is that whatever one does will make a lot of people furious. One cannot be consistent, and therefore one is an incompetent and worse. Any linguistic change troubles like new currency and stamps. Even God and his envoy Adam had trouble in naming and spelling in the Garden. In these often pained choices I have been helped hugely by my former colleague at Wesleyan University, William Mc-Culloh, with whom I collaborated for both *Greek Lyric Poetry* (1961) and *Sappho: Lyrics in the Original Greek and Translations* (1965). Now, as in the past, it is his scholarship against my amateurism. I learn from him. Mc-Culloh is absolute in making me note all sins. So what you find here may be enervating but not slipshod. Not on McCulloh's watch, for which I am endlessly grateful.

In general I prefer to be closer to what Italians do with *Cicero* and Greeks with *Euripides*. They pronounce all common words and ancient names as they do Italian and modern Greek and do not aspirate their φ. Hence, Greeks sitting in an ancient amphitheater or standing in an Orthodox church understand the old chanted Greek. Whatever script is used to record Sappho in another tongue, as she sings in Greek she must sing in English. The smallest of her surviving Greek fragments echoes with music.

If you hear some here, you may forgive the graphic signs.

W. B.

NOTES

1. Many scholars now call Longinos, the first-century author of *On the Sublime,* by the name Pseudo-Longinos to distinguish him from Cassius Longinos, a third-century author who through the nineteenth century was incorrectly believed to have composed this major treatise.

2. Some of those forms that she invented one could not see on papyrus as lineated verse, because the words were jammed together to save space. Those distinctions of lines and stanzas were the work of hellenistic rhetoricians in Alexandria centuries later.

3. One of these two poems, fragment 58, was first published in 1922, but this was only a partial translation, based on an incomplete Greek fragment. The complete version of the poem—so far as we can tell—was published in 2004 after the discovery of a third-century B.C.E. papyrus found in the Cologne University archives. Martin. L. West first published the find in Greek alone in the *Zeitschrift für Papyrologie und Epigraphik* 151 (2005), 1–9, and in Greek along with his English translation in the *Times Literary Supplement* (June 21, 2005, 1).

4. Mytilini was the major polis of ancient Lesbos. It is now the name of both the capital and the island. On modern maps, "Lesbos" often appears in parentheses and in modern Greek remains as an elegant synonym for "Mytilini" the island.

5. Just how prevalent the disguisement was, was proved to me one day in June of 1962, in Burgos, Spain. I had been working in the archives of the Spanish poet Manuel Machado, brother of Antonio Machado, to find information about don Antonio. I came upon a postcard to Manuel sent to him in the early 1930s by Miguel de Unamuno. Unamuno was a foremost Spanish novelist, poet, and philosopher, and also a classical scholar, maverick journalist, and then rector (president) of the University of Salamanca. In intellectual thought, Unamuno was and remains a grand world author, admired for his novelistic innovations that anticipate later postmodernism. His most famous exchange with history occurred in late August of 1936, when Francisco Franco's army took over Salamanca and its medieval university. At a meeting with the generals in his office, Unamuno denounced them, saying, "Vencerán tal vez pero no convencerán" (You may win but not convince). The response was shouts of "¡Muera la inteligencia!" (Let the intelligentsia die!). The philosopher was placed under house arrest, where he

remained till his death. Despite all of his enlight-
ened academic, creative, and courageous baggage,
Unamuno wrote in his card to Manuel Machado
that he had recently been rereading his Greek
Sappho, "not the one of the infamous reputation
but the true Sappho in the poems." Unamuno's
message was that whoever really knew Greek
knew that Sappho was *not* a lesbian.

6. See David A. Campbell, ed., *Greek Lyric Poetry: A
Selection* (London: Macmillan, 1967), 5n4..

7. The above description of the sapphic is crude,
omitting all reference to length of syllables (short
and long) and irregularities. For more see Denys
Page's "Appendix on Metres" in *Sappho and Al-
caeus: An Introduction to the Study of Ancient Lesbian
Poetry* (Oxford: Clarendon Press, 1979); *The Meters
of Greek and Latin Poetry* by Thomas G. Rosen-
meyer, James W. Halporn, and Martin Ostwald
(Indianapolis: Bobbs-Merrill, 1963); and the Metri-
cal Guide by William E. McCulloh at the end of
this book.

8. *Oratio ad graecos*, 53.

9. In the last few years our means of deciphering
both papyri and parchment texts have dramati-
cally increased as a result of X-rays and infrared
technology. At the Stanford Linear Accelerator
Center at Stanford University, a particle accel-
erator is being used to read a hitherto unreadable

tenth-century palimpsest containing a 174-page book of the mathematician Archimedes hidden below a Christian prayer book. The original writing was erased in order to record a Christian prayer book. By shooting X-rays at the parchment, the iron in the ink of the "erased" ancient text glows, revealing a now perfectly legible mathematic treatise under the later prayer book.

A parallel technological breakthrough is being used to decipher the literary elements of the some four hundred thousand Oxyrhynchus papyri fragments. Through multispectral imaging based on satellite imaging, the faded ink on ancient papyri comes clearly into view. English and American scientists and scholars have already deciphered lines from Sophocles's lost play *Epigonoi* (The Progeny), three pages in elegiac meter by the seventh-century lyric poet Archilochos, and works by Euripides, Hesiod, and Lucian. There is realistic hope that in coming years the amount of significant ancient texts, including early Gnostic and Christian scripture, may be increased by more than 20 percent. Hopefully, this translation of Sappho's works will soon be outdated when new strophes from the popular Lesbian poet are revealed. For extensive information, see POxy (Oxyrhynchus Online) at www.papyrology.ox.ac.uk.

10. In 1961, for the first time, a cache of eight original papyri, in poor condition, was found in continental Greece at Dervani (Lagada). See Herbert Hunger, "Papyrusfund in Griechenland," *Chronique d'Egypte* (Brussels) 37, no. 74 (July 1961).

11. Bowra modifies his defense of Sappho's "purity" in the 1961 edition of his *Greek Lyric Poetry,* by which time fellow scholars took a new line, acknowledging that Sappho's poems were indeed homoerotic.

12. William Mure of Caldwell, *A Critical History of the Language and Literature of Antient Greece,* 2nd ed., vol. 3 (London: Longman, Brown, Green, and Longmans, 1854), 315–16.

13. John Addington Symonds, *Studies of the Greek Poets* (London: Smith, Elder, & Co., 1873), 173.

14. Katherine Duncan-Jones, *Shakespeare's Sonnets* (London: Arden Shakespeare, 1997), 80–81.

15. The translation is by Aliki Barnstone in *The Collected Poems of C. P. Cavafy: A New Translation* (New York: W. W. Norton 2006), 36.

16. For an interesting and full examination of the condition of transport, see Marghanita Laski, *Ecstasy: A Study of Some Secular and Religious Experiences* (Bloomington: Indiana University Press, 1962).

17. For interested readers, a detailed list of sources can be found in *The Complete Poems of Sappho* (Boulder, CO: Shambhala Publications, 2009).

18. In Wade-Giles, if one knew the rules, which neither people nor dictionaries did, *Peking* was supposed to be pronounced *Beijing* because the unvoiced consonants *p* and *k* were to be voiced. Fat chance. Only when ungainly Pinyin took over did we have a clue about transcribing Mandarin (*putonghua*) into English. We are still stuck with *Tao* instead of *Dao*, though not for long.

AFRODITI OF THE
FLOWERS AT KNOSSOS

Prayer to Afroditi

On your dappled throne eternal Afroditi,
cunning daughter of Zeus,
I beg you, do not crush my heart
    with pain, O lady,

but come here if ever before
you heard my voice from far away,
and yielding left your father's house
    of gold and came,

yoking birds to your chariot. Beautiful
quick sparrows whirring on beating wings
took you from heaven down to mid sky
    over the black earth

and soon arrived. O blessed one,
on your deathless face a smile,
you asked me what I am suffering
    and why I call you,

what I most want to happen
in my crazy heart. "Whom shall I persuade
again to take you into her love? Who,
    O Psapfo, wrongs you?

If she runs away, soon she will pursue.
If she scorns gifts, now she will bribe.
If she doesn't love, soon she will love
     even unwillingly."

Come to me now and loosen me
from blunt agony. Labor
and fill my heart with fire. Stand by me
     and be my ally.

[1]

Afroditi of the
Flowers at Knossos

Leave Kriti and come here to this holy
temple with your graceful grove
of apple trees and altars smoking
        with frankincense.

Icy water babbles through apple branches
and roses leave shadow on the ground
and bright shaking leaves pour down
        profound sleep.

Here is a meadow where horses graze
amid wild blossoms of the spring and soft winds
        blow aroma

of honey. Afroditi, take the nectar
and delicately pour it into gold
wine cups and mingle joy with
        our celebration.

[2]

Moon and Women

The moon appeared in her fullness
when women took their place around the altar

[154]

Dancers at a Kritan Altar

Kritan women once danced supplely
around a beautiful altar with light feet,

crushing the soft flowers of grass.

[16   Incert.]

In Time of Storm

Brightness

and with good luck
we will reach the harbor
and black earth

We sailors have no will
in big blasts of wind,
hoping for dry land

and to sail
our cargo
floating about

Many
labors
until dry land

[20]

To Lady Hera

Be near me Lady Hera while I pray
for your graceful form to appear,
to which the sons of Atreus prayed,
those dazzling kings

who did bountiful deeds,
first at Troy, then on the sea,
but sailing the road to this island,
they could not reach it

till they called on you and Zeus god of
    suppliants,
and Dionysos lovely son of Thyoni.
Now be gentle and help me too
as in old days,

holy and beautiful
virgin
in circles

to sail safely
to the shrine

[17]

INVITATION

Invitation for one
not all
to come to a feast

for Hera   accomplishing
as long
as
I am alive

[9]

SACRIFICE

To you I will pour wine

over flesh of a white goat

[40   INCERT. (13)]

Death of Adonis

Afroditi, delicate Adonis is dying.
                    What should we do?

Virgins, beat your breasts
                    and tear your garments.

[140]

Adonis Gone

O for Adonis!

[168]

To Afroditi

O gold-crowned Afroditi,
if only I could win this lot!

[33]

AFRODITI

Queen
to you
a horse

[87e, f]

AFRODITI TO PSAPFO

Both you Psapfo and my servant Eros

[159]

Days of Harshness

Quiet
Zeus
of the goatskin shield

and Kythereia
I pray

holding a good heart,
and if ever

like other days when you left Kypros,
hear my prayer

and come
to my
severities

[86]

Artemis on Solitary Mountains

Gold-haired Phoebus borne by Koios's daughter
after she joined with Kronos's son Zeus god of
    high clouds
        and high name.
Artemis swore the great oath of the gods to
    Zeus:
"By your head, I shall always be a virgin
untamed, hunting on peaks of solitary
    mountains.
Come, grant me this grace!"
So she spoke. Then the father of the blessed gods
nodded his consent. Now gods and mortals
call her by her thrilling eponym, *The Virgin Deer
    Hunter.*
Eros, loosener of limbs, never comes near her

[44a]

Artemis

blame
delicate
Artemis

[84]

NIGHTINGALE

Evening Star

Hesperos, you bring home all the bright dawn
scattered,
bring home the sheep,
bring home the goat, bring the child home
to her mother.

[104a]

Hesperos

Of all stars the most beautiful

[104b]

Moon

Stars around the beautiful moon
conceal their luminous form
when in her fullness she shines
        on the earth

in silver

[34]

EARTH

Earth is embroidered
with rainbow-colored garlands

[168c]

NIGHTINGALE

Nightingale with your lovely voice
you are the herald of spring

[136]

CICADA

Flaming summer
charms the earth with its own fluting,
and under leaves
the cicada scrapes its tiny wings together
and incessantly
pours out full shrill song

[101a]

Doves Playing Dead

When their souls grew cold they dropped
their wings to their sides

[42]

Of Gello Who Died Young, Whose Ghost Haunts Little Children

She was even fonder
of children than Gello.

[178]

World

I could not hope
to touch the sky
with my two arms

[52]

Eos

Lady Dawn

[157]

Dawn

Suddenly
Dawn in gold sandals

[123]

WALKING TO A WEDDING

Hair Yellower Than Torch Flame

My mother used to say

in her youth
it was a great ornament to wear
a purple ribbon

looped in her hair. But a girl
with hair yellower than torch flame
need wear just

a wreath of blooming
flowers, or lately maybe
a colorful headband

from Sardis
or some Ionian city

[98a]

Time of Youth

You will
remember
we did these things
in our youth,

many and beautiful things.

In the city
for us the harsh

We live
Opposite

a daring
person

stone foundation
thin-voiced

[24a, b, c]

Of a Young Lover

When I was young I wove garlands

[125]

My Daughter

I have a beautiful child like a gold flower
in form. I wouldn't trade
my darling Kleis for all Lydia or lovely . . .

[132]

Wildflowers

A tender girl picking wildflowers

[122]

The Virgin

Like a sweet apple reddening on a high branch,
on the tip of the topmost branch and forgotten
by the apple pickers—no, beyond their reach.

Like a hyacinth in the mountains that shepherd
    men
trample down with their feet, and on the earth
the purple flower

[105a, c]

Girl

A sweet-voiced girl

[153]

Remorse

Do I still long for my virginity?

[107]

Words with Virginity

Virginity, virginity, where have you gone,
  leaving me abandoned?
No longer will I come to you. No longer will I
  come.

[114]

The Lyre Speaks

Tell of the bride with beautiful feet
let Artemis

the violet-robed daughter of Zeus
let the violet-robed put aside her anger.

Come holy Graces and Pierian Muses
when songs are in the heart
listening to a clear song

The bridegroom   annoying   companions

her hair   placing the lyre

Dawn with gold sandals

[103]

Wedding of Andromache and Hektor

From Kypros
a herald came
Idaos the swift-running Trojan messenger

telling of the wedding's imperishable fame in all
    Asia:
"Hektor and his companions are bringing
    dancing-eyed
delicate Andromache on ships over the salt sea
from holy Thibai and Plakia's flowing waters
along with many gold bracelets and purple
fragrant clothes, exquisite adornments
and countless silver cups and ivory."

He spoke, and Hektor's dear father sprang to his
    feet
and news spread to friends throughout the
    spacious city.
Instantly the sons of Ilos, founder of Troy,
yoked mules to carriages with smooth-running
    wheels,
and a whole crowd of women and slender-ankled
    virgins
        climbed aboard.

The daughters of Priamos came in their own
    carts,
and young unmarried men yoked stallions to
    chariots.
In great spirit
charioteers

                          moved like gods
                          holy all together
and set out   for Ilion
in a confusion of sweet-voiced flutes and kithara
and small crashing castanets,
and young virgins sang a loud heavenly song
whose amazing echo pierced the ether of
    the sky.
Everywhere in the streets
were bowls and cups.
Myrrh and cassia and frankincense rode on the
    wind.

Old women shouted in happiness
and all the men sang out with thrilling force,
calling on far-shooting Paean Apollo nimble on
    the lyre
and sang to godlike Hektor and Andromache.

                                                [44]

WALKING TO A WEDDING

Yes you were once a child
come sing these things
talk to us and give us
     your grace

We are walking to a wedding, and surely
you know too, but quickly as you can
send the young virgins away. May gods
     have

Yet for men   road to
     great Olympos

[27]

SONG TO THE GROOM

What are you like, lovely bridegroom?
You are most like a slender sapling.

[115]

Song for the Bride

O bridegroom, there is no other woman now
        like her

[113]

Lesbian Bride

O beautiful, O graceful girl

[108]

Guarding the Bride

Take care of her
O bridegrooms
O kings of cities!

[161]

Chamber

Room
the bride with her beautiful feet
now
for me

[103b]

Hermis at a Wedding

There a bowl of ambrosia
was mixed, and Hermis
took the jug and poured wine for the gods
and then they all
held out cups and poured
libations and prayed for all blessings
for the groom.

[141a, b]

FRAGMENTS

Carry

Arheanassa

once

in lovely

heard

virgins

of the springs

[103C, a, b]

To Hymen, Wedding God

High! Raise the roof!
O Hymen.
Lift it up, carpenters!
O Hymen.
The bridegroom is coming, the equal of Aris,
O Hymen.
taller than a giant!
O Hymen!

[111]

Song to Groom and Bride

Happy groom, your marriage you prayed for
has happened. You have the virgin bride
of your prayer.

You the bride are a form of grace,
your eyes honey.
Desire rains on your exquisite face.

Afroditi has honored you exceedingly

[112]

Night Song

Night

Virgins
will all night long sing
of the love between you and your bride
in her violet robe.

Wake and call out young men
of your age,
and tonight we shall sleep less than
the bright-voiced nightingale

[30]

A Guard outside the Bridal Chamber, Who Keeps the Bride's Friends from Rescuing Her

The doorkeeper's feet are seven fathoms long.
It took five oxhides for his sandals
and ten shoemakers to cobble them together.

[110]

END OF A PARTY

Beautiful
he throws peace into frenzy
and exhaustion and dumbs the mind.
Sitting

But come, my friends.
Soon daybreak.

[43 (lines 3–9)]

YOU BURN US

Seizure

To me he seems equal to gods,
the man who sits facing you
and hears you near as you speak
    softly and laugh

in a sweet echo that jolts
the heart in my ribs. Now
when I look at you a moment
    my voice is empty

and can say nothing as my tongue
cracks and slender fire races
under my skin. My eyes are dead
    to light, my ears

pound, and sweat pours over me.
I convulse, greener than grass
and feel my mind slip as I go
    close to death.

Yet I must suffer, even poor

[31]

39

Alone

The moon has set and
the Pleiades. Middle
of the night, time spins
away and I lie alone.

[168b]

Emptiness

Never have I found you more repulsive,
O Irana.

[91]

Eros

Love shook my heart like wind
on a mountain punishing oak trees.

[47]

Love

Eros came out of heaven,
dressed in a purple cape

[54]

SUPREME SIGHT ON THE BLACK EARTH

Some say cavalry and others claim
infantry or a fleet of long oars
is the supreme sight on the black earth.
          I say it is

the one you love. And easily proved.
Didn't Helen, who far surpassed
all in beauty, desert the best of men
          her husband and king

and sail off to Troy and forget
her daughter and dear parents? Merely
love's gaze made her bend
          and led her

from her path.
These tales
remind me now of Anaktoria
          who is gone.

And I would rather see her supple step
and motion of light on her face
than chariots of the Lydians or ranks
          of foot soldiers in bronze.

Now this is impossible
yet among the living I pray for a share

unexpectedly.

[16]

To Eros

You burn us

[38]

Absence

I long and yearn for

[36]

Goatherd

Goatherd
a rose

longing

sweat

[74a (lines 2, 4); 74b (line 2); 74c (line 2)]

Shall I?

I don't know what to do.
I think yes—and then no.

[51]

Pleasure

On a soft pillow
I will lay down my limbs

[46]

Encounter

Finding something
desires
Carry out a plan
suddenly
I call out from my heart.
for all you want to win
fight for me
persuaded by a voluptuous woman
as you know very well

[60]

Homecoming

You came and I went mad about you.
You cooled my mind burning with longing.

[48]

Desire

Nor
desire
but together
a flower
desire
I was happy

[78]

A God

And this
disastrous
god

I swear did not love
but now because

and the cause neither
nothing much

[67a]

ABSENT

Away
from her

yet she became
like gods

sinful Andromeda
a blessed one

didn't hold back
her insolence

sons of Tyndareus
gracious

no longer innocent
Megara

[68a]

Of Those Unwilling to Take the Bitter with the Sweet

I care for neither honey
nor the honeybee

[146]

Endure

Bring about?

I want
to hang on
she said

[76]

I Shall

As long as you want to

[45]

RETURN, GONGYLA

To a Friend Gone, Remember

Honestly I wish I were dead.
When she left me she wept

profusely and told me,
"Oh how we've suffered in all this.
Psapfo, I swear I go unwillingly."

And I answered her,
"Be happy, go and remember me,
you know how we worshipped you.

But if not, I want
to remind you
of beautiful days we shared,

how you took wreaths of violets,
roses and crocuses,
and at my side

tied them in garlands
made of flowers
round your tender throat,

and with sweet myrrh oil
worthy of a queen
you anointed your limbs

and on a soft bed
gently   you would satisfy
your longing

and how there was no
holy shrine
where we were absent,

no grove
no dance
no sound"

[94]

Beauty in a Man

A man who is beautiful is beautiful to see
but a good man at once takes on beauty.

[50]

Atthis

I loved you Atthis once long ago.

You seemed to me a little child and graceless.

[49]

Her Friends

For you the beautiful ones my thought
    is unchangeable

[41]

Sweetbitter

Eros loosener of limbs once again trembles me,
a sweetbitter beast irrepressibly creeping in

[130]

Return, Gongyla

A deed
your lovely face

if not, winter
and no pain

I bid you, Abanthis,
take up the lyre
and sing of Gongyla as again desire
floats around you

the beautiful. When you saw her dress
it excited you. I'm happy.
The Kypros-born once
blamed me

for praying
this word:
I want

[22]

You Can Free Me

I hoped for love

When I look at you face to face
not even Hermioni
seems to be your equal.
I compare you to blond Helen

among mortal women.
Know that you can free me
from every care,

and stay awake all night long
on dewy riverbanks

[23]

KYDRO

I'm waiting
to offer you a good thing
in sacrifices

but going there
we know
is labor

later toward
Kydro say
I am coming

[19]

You in Sardis

In Sardis
her thoughts turn constantly to us here,

to you like a goddess. She was happiest
in your song.

Now she shines among Lydian women
as after sunset
the rosy-fingered moon

surpasses all the stars, and her light reaches
equally across the salt sea
and over meadows steeped in flowers.

Lucent dew pours out profusely
on blooming roses,
on frail starflowers and florid honey clover.

But wandering back and forth she remembers
gentle Atthis and for your pain
a heavy yearning consumes her

but to go there
the mind
endlessly is singing

[96 (lines 1–20)]

Afroditi and Desire

It is not easy for us to equal
the goddesses
in beauty of form Adonis

desire
and
Afroditi

poured nectar from
a gold pitcher
with hands Persuasion

the Geraistion shrine
lovers
of no one

I shall enter desire

[96 (lines 21–37)]

A Handsome Man

Stand and face me, my love,
and scatter the grace in your eyes

[138]

Myths

All would
say
that my tongue
tells tales

and for a greater
man

[18]

Paralysis

Sweet mother, now I cannot work the loom.
Sleek Afroditi broke me with longing for a boy.

[102]

Behind a Laurel Tree

You lay in wait
behind a laurel tree

and everything
was sweeter

women
wandering

I barely heard
darling soul

such as I now am
you came

beautiful
in your garments

[62]

Companions

For my companions,
now of these things I shall sing beautifully

[160]

Lito and Niobi

Lito and Niobi were deep friends

[142]

As Long As There Is Breath

You might wish
a little
to be carried off

Someone
sweeter
you also know

forgot

and would say
yes
I shall love   as long as there is breath in me
and care
I say I have been a strong lover

hurt
bitter
and know this

no matter
I shall love

   [88a (lines 5–11, 13–17, 19–20, 22–24); b (line 15)]

Return

I have flown to you like a child to her mother.

[25   Incert.]

WEATHERCOCKS AND EXILE

Fury

When anger is flooding through your chest
best to quiet your reckless barking tongue

[158]

Abuse

Often
those
I treat well are just the ones
who most harm me
vainly

You I want
to suffer
In me
I know it

[26 (lines 1–5, 9–12)]

GORGO

By now they have had enough of Gorgo

[144]

ANDROMEDA

Andromeda in a beautiful exchange,

"Psapfo, why ignore Afroditi rich in blessings?"

[133a, b]

ATTHIS DISAPPEARING

Atthis, now the mere thought of me
is hateful and you fly off to Andromeda

[131]

Where Am I?

But you have forgotten me

or you love some man more than me

[129a, b]

A Ring

Crazy woman
why are you bragging to me about a ring?

Madden

Don't madden
my mind

Delicate Girl

Delicate girl
once again
I leaped
and wandered

[5a, b, c   Incert.]

Andromeda, What Now?

What farm girl dolled up in a farm dress
captivates your wits
not knowing how to pull her rags down to her
    ankles?

[57]

Hello and Goodbye

A hearty good day to the daughter of the house
     of Polyanax

[155]

Mika

You have done wrong, Mika,
I won't allow you to

faithless you chose love in the house
of Penthilos

A sweet song
in honey voice
sings
clear nightingales
over dew fields

[71]

Alkaios Speaks and Psapfo Responds

"I want to say something to you but shame
disarms me"

"If you longed for the good or beautiful
and your tongue were not concocting evil,
shame would not cover your eyes.
Rather you would speak about the just,"

[137]

In My Pain

My pain drips

May terrifying winds carry off him
who blames me

[37]

From Her Exile

For you Kleis I have no embroidered
headband and no idea
where to find one while the Mytilinian rules

These colorfully embroidered
headbands

these things of the children of the Kleanax
In exile
memories terribly wasted away

[98b]

PROTECT MY BROTHER HARAXOS

O Kypris and Nereids, I pray you
to sail my brother home unharmed
and let him accomplish all
      that is in his heart

and be released from former error
and carry joy to his friends
and bane to enemies and let no one
      bring us more grief.

Let him honor me his sister.
But black torment
      suffering for early days,

citizens accused.
Was it over millet seed?

Pure Kypris, put aside
old anger and free him from
      evil sorrow

                            [5]

To My Brother Haraxos

By giving

good fame
your beauty and nobility
to such friends
you sicken me with pain

Blame you? Swollen
Have your fill of them
For my thinking it is poorly done
and all night I understand baseness

Other
Minds
the blessed

[3]

TO AFRODITI ABOUT HER BROTHER'S LOVER

Blessed one

May he be released from his past wrongs
with luck
now in harbor

Kypris, may she feel your sharp needles
and may she Doriha not go on crowing
how he came back a second time
to his desired love.

[15]

DORIHA

Doriha
commands them
not to come

she is arrogant
like young men
who are loved

[7]

SECRET OF MY CRAFT

Holy Tortoise Shell

Come holy lyre speak to me
and become a voice!

[118]

Some Honored Me

Some honored me by giving me
the secret of their works

[32]

Graces

Holy Graces with arms of roses,
come to me, daughters of Zeus

[53]

Singer

Towering is the Lesbian singer
compared to those in other lands

[106]

Graces and Muses

Come to me now tender Graces
and Muses with beautiful hair

[128]

The Muses

Muses come here again to me
leaving the gold house

[127]

Happiness

Wealth without virtue is no harmless neighbor
but by mixing both you are on the peak of joy.

[148]

Light

I cannot imagine in the future any girl
who looks on the light of the sun
who will have your skill and wisdom.

[56]

SANDAL

A Swan's Egg Containing
Kastor and Polydeukis

They say that Lida once found an egg
hidden and the color of hyacinth

[166]

Comparisons

Far sweeter in sound than a lyre
more golden than gold

far whiter than an egg

[156, 167]

A Swallow

O Irana, why is King Pandion's daughter
now a swallow waking me?

[135]

Jason's Cloak

A mingling of all kinds of colors

[152]

Robe

robe
colored with saffron

purple robe
cloak

garland crowns
beauty

Phrygian purple
rugs

[92]

Chickpeas

Gold broom grew on riverbanks

[143]

Purple Handcloth

These purple handcloths
perfumed
she sent you from Phokaia
are expensive gifts

[101]

Beauty of Her Friends

Mnasidika is more beautifully formed
than even soft Gyrinno

[82a]

ON GOING BAREHEADED

Rebuff other ways
as quickly as you can

and you, Dika, with your soft hands take stems
of lovely anise and loop them in your locks.

The blessed Graces love to gaze at one in flowers
but turn their backs on one whose hair is bare.

[81]

SANDAL

Colorful straps covered
her feet
in beautiful Lydian work

[39]

GARMENT

She was wrapped all around with a delicate
woven cloth

[100]

DREAM AND SLEEP

Dawn with Gold Arms

Go
so we can see
Lady Dawn
with gold arms.
Doom

[6 (lines 7, 8, 10, 11, 14)]

Sleep

May you sleep
on your tender girlfriend's breasts

[126]

Black Sleep

When all night long
   sleep closes down

and the eyes the black sleep of night

[149, 151]

In a Dream

In a dream I talked with you born in Kypros

[134]

Dream

O dream on black wings
you stray here when sleep

sweet god, I am in agony
to split all its power

for I expect not to share.
Nothing of the blessed gods

I would rather not be like this
with trinkets

but may
I have them all

[63]

INNOCENCE

I am not of a wounding spirit
rather I have a gentle heart

[120]

CLEAR VOICED

I will go
hear
harmony
dance choir
clear voiced
to all

[70 (lines 3, 7, 9–11, 13)]

Dew

Afroditi
soft-worded desires
hurl
holding
a seat

flourishing
lovely
dew

[73a]

Face

Now in my
heart I
see clearly

a beautiful
face
shining back on me,

stained
with love

[4]

AGE AND LIGHT

Old Man

Rich
like listening to
an old man

[85]

Gods

Among gods
right off
the one
who sheds
no tears

[139]

Angry with Her Daughter
When She Psapfo Was Dying

It is not right in a house serving the Muses
to have mourning. For us it is unbecoming.

[150]

OLD AGE

In pity
and
trembling

old age now
covers my flesh.
Yet there is chasing and floating

after a young woman.
Pick up your lyre
and sing to us

of one with violets
on her robe, especially
wandering

[21]

No Oblivion

Someone, I tell you, in another time,
will remember us.

[147]

To Hermis Who Guides the Dead

Gongyla

surely a sign
especially for children
who came here

I said, O master   by the blessed
Afroditi   I swear I take no pleasure
in being on the earth

but a longing seizes me to die
and see the dewy
lotus banks of the Aheron

[95]

To a Woman of No Education

When you lie dead no one will remember
or long for you later. You do not share the roses
of Pieria. Unseen here and in the house of
    Hades,
flown away, you will flitter among dim corpses.

                          [55]

Menelaos

He lies received in the black earth,
a son of Atreus,
released now from his agony.

                [27   Incert. (1)]

Wish

Both distress and good health

My children, let me fly back
youth.

[18b, c   Incert.]

Age and the Bed

Really, if you are my friend,
       choose a younger bed
I can't bear to live with you
       when I am the older

[121]

Afroditi to Psapfo

Andromeda
forgot

but Psapfo
I loved you

In Kypros I am queen
for you a power

as sun blazes
glory everywhere;

even by the Aheron I am with you

[65]

Growing Old[*]

Those lovely gifts of the fragrant-breasted
    Muses,
girls, seek them eagerly in thrilling song of the
    lyre.

Old age has grasped my earlier delicate skin
and my black hair has become white,

my spirit turned heavy, my knees no longer
carry me nimble for dancing like a fawn.

About these things I groan. What can I do?
For a human not to grow old is impossible.

They say Dawn, dazzled by love, took Tithonos
in her rose arms to the utter end of the earth.

Once beautiful and young, time seized him
into gray old age, husband of a deathless wife.

                                                    [58b]

[*] Translated by Willis Barnstone and William McCulloh.

Desire and Sun

Yet I love refinement and Eros has got me
brightness and the beauty of the sun.

[58c (lines 25–26)]

INDIRECT POEMS

Death Is Evil

Death is evil. So the gods decided.
Otherwise they would die.

ARISTOTLE, *RHETORIC* 1398B

[201]

Gold

Gold is indestructible.

SCHOLIAST ON PINDAR'S
PYTHIAN ODES 4.410C
(II.153 DRACHMANN)

[204]

ELEGIAC POEMS FROM THE
GREEK ANTHOLOGY WRONGLY
ATTRIBUTED TO SAPPHO

On Pelagon

Pelagon the fisherman. His father Meniskos left
    here
        his basket and oar, relics of a wretched life.

[159 Diehl]

On Timas

Here is the dust of Timas who unmarried
        was led into Persefoni's dark bedroom,
and when she died her girlfriends took sharp
        iron knives and cut off their soft hair.

[158 Diehl]

GLOSSARY

When numbers appear at the end of an entry, they indicate poems in which the glossary term appears.

Abanthis Nothing is known of Abanthis. 22.

Adonis A handsome young god of vegetation and fertility. Because of his beauty, both Afroditi and Persefoni (Persephone) coveted young Adonis as a lover. He was identified with the seeding and harvesting of crops and was worshiped especially by women. When Adonis was killed by the tusks of a wild boar, Afroditi and Persefoni each wanted him as her lover. Zeus intervened and assigned him to spend half the year with Afroditi aboveground in the summer months and the other half with Persefoni down in Hades. Other versions give Adonis four months with each of the courting women and four months alone or with his choice companion. Adonis's death and resurrection were celebrated in festivals in Greece as a symbol of the yearly cycle of vegetation. Some say that the boar that killed Adonis was sent by his lover, the chaste Artemis, or by her lover, Aris, who was jealous of Adonis's beauty. Each drop of Adonis's blood turned into a blood red flower, the anemone.

Adonis as a lord of fertility goes back to Meso-
potamian roots, including his worship among the
Phrygians as Attis and among the Babylonians as
Tammuz. The word *adonis* means "lord," a Semitic
word found in Aramaic and Hebrew that has en-
tered many Indo-European languages. In the He-
brew Bible *adonai* means "my lord" and is, along
with Yahweh (the tetragrammaton YHWH) and
Ha Shem (the name), a name for nameless God. In
Spanish, *don,* from *adonis,* is a male honorific title,
as in Don Quijote, and *donaña* is a feminine title, as
in Doña Perfecta. In Italian, *adonis* has given us the
honorifics *donna* and *donatello* (little lord). 140, 168.

Afroditi (Aphrodite; Afrodita in Sappho's Aiolic speech)
A goddess of love, beauty, sea, flowers, and fertil-
ity. In Homer, Afroditi is the daughter of Zeus and
Dioni. She was born in the sea foam (*afros*) off the
shore of Paphos in Kypros (Cyprus), but that froth
consisted of blood and semen dropped into the sea
after Kronos castrated Ouranos (Uranus), god of
the sky. To keep her in check, Zeus compelled the
goddess of desire to marry the ugly Hefaistos (Hep-
hestus), the god of fire and the forge, who is Vulcan
in Roman mythology. Afroditi was bored with the
metalworker. When Hefaistos found her and Aris
in a lovers' embrace, he locked them in an iron net.
But from her union with Aris she bore Harmona
and, in some versions, also Anteros and Eros. By

Hermis she bore Hermafroditos, and by Dionysos she was the mother of phallic Priapos. The Romans inherited a deific past when Zeus caused her to fall in love with the shepherd Anchises, whose offspring was Aeneas, the later Roman hero. Her star affair was with the beautiful youth Adonis, whom Persefoni also desired. Zeus arranged for the jealous goddesses to share Adonis, giving six (or four) months' possession to each.

Afroditi had an important cult at Kythera on Kriti (see poems 2, 86, and 140). She was often accompanied by her son Eros, also a god of love and desire. As a symbol of passion and romantic love, she is a particular ally to Sappho and is mentioned by Sappho in the existing fragments more often than any other deity or person. The complete poem attributed to Sappho (fragment 1) is addressed to Afroditi. Sappho calls her variously Kypris (Cypris), Kyprian (Cyprian), Kypros-born (Cyprus-born), the Pafian (Paphian) of Pafos (Paphos), and Kythereia.

Earlier, in Mesopotamia, she was Astarte and Ishtar, while in Rome she was Venus. 1; 2; 33; 44; 65; 73a; 87e, f; 95; 96; 101; 102; 112; 133a, b; 159; 168.

Aheron (Acheron) The river of death running through Hades. It began in Thesprotia, Epeiros, and disappeared underground in places where it was supposed to lead to Hades. *Aheron* is frequently a synonym of *Hades.* 95.

Alkaios (Alcaeus) Born about 620 B.C.E. in Mytilini (Lesbos), the poet was a contemporary and possible friend or lover of Sappho's. He wrote, in the Aiolic (Lesbian) dialect, lyric poems that deal with politics, love, drinking, the sea. The ship-of-state poem, made famous by Horace, is earliest found in the poems of Alkaios. The best-known modern version is Walt Whitman's "Oh Captain, My Captain," whose origin goes directly back to Lesbian Alkaios. Alkaios was of an aristocratic family in Lesbos, and when the enemy Pittakos became the tyrant (ruler), Alkaios and his family went into exile. 137.

Anaktoria One of Sappho's friends. One theory is that she left Sappho in order to marry and follow her husband to Sardis, where he was probably a soldier. 16.

Andromache (Andromáhi) Her name is composed of *andros,* meaning "man," and *máhi,* meaning "battle" or "war." She was the wife of Hektor, the Trojan hero, who was killed by Achilles. Later the princess widow married Hektor's brother Helenos, and they ruled jointly in Epeiros (Epirus), present-day northwestern Greece and Albania. Homer is evenhanded in treating Achaians and Trojans, portraying Andromache as a noble figure. Sappho celebrates her, and she is the tragic heroine of plays by Euripides and Racine. 44.

Andromeda A rival of Sappho's; perhaps a poet. 68a; 131; 133a, b.

Apollo Apollo the sun god and his twin sister Artemis
the moon god were born in Delos, the children of
Zeus and Lito (Leto). He was a god of prophecy,
music, medicine, archery. He was also the ideal of
young, manly beauty, and connected with philoso-
phy and all the arts. For mystery religions and gnos-
ticism, he was Phoebus, the god of light.

Apollo failed in his attempt to seduce Dafni
(Daphne), known as Laura to the Romans. Dafni
turned herself into a laurel tree (*dafni,* in Greek)
rather than yield to him. He ran off like a lowly
hound, as Ovid writes, but fooled himself into be-
lieving himself victorious by seizing leaves of the
laurel tree and crowning himself with them as a
sign of his conquest: hence, the Olympic laurel
leaves today signify victory.

There were many shrines to worship the sun
god, the major oracular and athletic one being at
Delfi, where the Pythian Games were held in his
honor every four years. Apollo is above all identi-
fied with perfection, beauty, and art. In this he was
the leader of the Muses, directing their choir. His
attributes included the lyre (cithara) and plectrum,
as well as swans, wolves, dolphins, and bows and
arrows. The "far-shooting archer" was one of his
titles. He was also a god of prophecy and medi-
cine. In literature his golden-mean qualities are of-
ten contrasted to those of his brother Dionysos. In

The Birth of Tragedy, Nietzsche contrasts Dionysian madness and inspiration to Apollonian measure, harmony, and reason.

Sappho's poem on the wedding of Andromache and Hektor ends with a thrilling paean, which is a hymn sung to Apollo. Among Apollo's many epithets were Phoebus and Paean. Sappho called him Paon, the Aiolic form of Paean (Paian). 44.

Aris (Ares) Aris, the fierce Olympian war god, was the son of Zeus and Hera, though in one legend he and his twin sister, Eris, were born when Hera touched a flower. He fought gods and mortals. When Poseidon's son violated Aris's daughter, Aris killed him. For his crime he was brought to trial and acquitted before a tribunal of twelve Olympians on a hill in Athens, later named for him, the Areiópagos (from *Areios págos,* the hill of Aris). The station of tribunals and juries was so strong in ancient Greece that even gods were brought before litigious prosecutors. Many later figures bear the name Areopagite, including Dionysios the Areopagite, whom Paul (Shaul) in Acts 17:34 converted on this hill named for the war god.

In the *Iliad,* Aris was fighting on the Trojan side. When Hera spotted him, she persuaded Zeus to have him wounded with a spear, after which he retreated to Mount Olympos. The worship of Aris as a god of war was not significant in Greece, but in

Rome, as mighty Mars, the cult of the god of power and empire was widespread. III.

Artemis Twin sister of Apollo, the virgin moon goddess of forest and hunt, of healing and childbirth. Artemis's own birth is a foremost legend. When Hera discovered that her consort Zeus had made Lito (Leto) pregnant, she forbade Lito to bear her children (who would be Artemis and Apollo) on the mainland. The islands were also fearful of accepting the tainted Lito, but the floating island of Delos, treasure-house of Athens, agreed to receive her. Then Zeus secured the island to the sea bottom with four great pillars or, in another version, by means of alabaster chains. The islands floating around Delos, the Cyclades, were called white swans. They were held up by floating turtles. As Artemis's island, Delos was a holy island, on which no one could be born or die.

When the hunter Aktaion (Actaeon) discovered Artemis naked and saw her ravishing beauty, Artemis turned him into a wild stag, which his own hounds tore apart and ate. As for the story of the virgin goddess's love affair with Aris, it is suspect. There were other men whom she was involved with, particularly Orion and Adonis, each of whom met his doom. Artemis's attribute beasts were the bear and the goat. Her central concern was virginity and the nymphs whom she trained to follow her, yet her representation in sculpture was often intensely sexual. The famous extant temple in Efesos contains a uniquely striking marble sculpture, whose torso is covered by erotic bumps that have been seen as large female nipples or bull testicles.

Artemis was also associated with the moon goddess Selini (Selene), who in later legend largely replaced her. In Rome Artemis was worshiped as Diana. 44a.

Atreidai (Atreidae) The Atreidai, usually referring to Agamemnon and Menelaos (Menelaus), are the descendants of Atreus. 27 incert.

Atreus Atreus was a king of Mykinai and father of Agamemnon and Menelaos. When his brother Thyestis tricked him into losing his throne, which he could only regain by reversing the track of the sun, he sought the aid of Zeus. Zeus made the sun move backward, and Atreus regained his throne. *See also* Atreidai.

Atthis One of Sappho's friends, treated with deep affection in many poems. Like Anaktoria (q.v.), she leaves Sappho. 49, 96, 131.

Dika Probably short for Mnasidika (q.v.), one of Sappho's friends. 81.

Dionysos (Dionysius) Also called Bakhos (Bacchus, by the Romans) and Zagreus, the god of Orphism. A god of vegetation, wine, and spiritual ecstasy, he was worshipped with orgiastic rites and often represents the counterpart of Apollonian moderation. Dionysos was also a civilizing figure, a lawgiver, peacemaker, and protector of the theater and the other arts. But his lasting fame was as god of divine imagination and of wild and frenzied creativity.

In the Olympian tradition, Dionysos was the son of Zeus and Persefoni. He was also said to be the child of Zeus and Semili (Semele). The strange tale of his birth inspired mystery religions centering on this Orphic figure, as well as later plays, operas, and paintings. Zeus impregnated Semili, a mortal. Jealous Hera was furious when she discovered from Semili her affair with Zeus. Hera caused Semili's death, but Zeus rescued the fetal Dionysos by sewing him into his thigh, and a few months later, Dionysos was born.

After his birth, Dionysos was brought up by rain nymphs on Mount Nysa. The gifted boy soon invented the art of wine making. Hera, however, could not forgive his being sired by Zeus and struck him with madness, whereupon he became a wanderer in many lands. In Phrygia, Rhea cured him and taught him religious rites. Then he spent years in India, refining his philosophical resources, and bringing his secrets of wine making to many places in Asia. When he returned, satyrs, maenads, and nymphs followed him, and festivals of dance, song, wine, and ecstatic transcendence were celebrated to honor him. But his very knowledge of wine, the esoteric, and mystery rites frightened the more temperate, who dreaded the possibility of madness that art and ecstasy might bring with it.

Perhaps no Greek god other than Apollo has had so constant and profound an influence on all fields as the Dionysian deity. In Nietzsche's *Birth of Tragedy,* the philosopher compares the two tendencies in the Greek drama, the Dionysian, that of the ecstatic creator, with its peaks and pits, and the Apollonian, whose even virtues bring equanimity and refined insight. These attributes may apply to the baroque and romantic versus the archaic and classical, be it art, philosophy, or letters. There have been mystics, saints, and magicians who bore Dionysos's name. Apollo may have been Sappho's meter, but Dionysos was her love friend of dance mysteries and song, of beauty's summits and desolation's chasms. 17.

Dioskouroi (Dioscuri) Kastor (Castor) and Polydeukis (Pollux), the sons of Tyndareus, were twin hero warriors in Sparta after whom the constellation Dioscuri (Castor and Pollux) was named; they are its brightest stars. Kastor was a horseman, Polydeukis a boxer. Though they were "twins" through their mother, they had different fathers, Kastor being the son of Lida (Leda) and Tyndareus, and Polydeukis the son of Lida and Zeus, though often they

are both identified as sons or descendents of King
Tyndareus of Sparta. Their sisters were Helen and
Klytemnestra. After Kastor died, he entreated Zeus
to let Polydeukis share with him his own immortal-
ity, and Zeus arranged for them to divide their time
between the night sky and dark Hades. He created
a constellation for them alone called Gemini (Latin
for "twins"), and they remain the patron stars of
sailors. 166.

Doriha (Doricha) Probably a girlfriend of Sappho's
brother Haraxos. 7; 15a, b.

Eros God of love, child or attendant of Afroditi. Sap-
pho makes Eros the son of Gaia (Ge, Earth) and
Ouranos (Sky), but she most often uses *eros* to mean
simply love that yearns for beauty, and especially for
sexual union.

Sappho describes Eros as sweetbitter and cruel
to victims. Eros is not really the boy god but his
metaphorical attribute: eros as difficult or joyous
love and its erotic flame. Sappho, however, did not
make this distinction in capital and lowercase let-
ters, since ancient scrolls ran unpunctuated words
together in capital letters. For her, Eros was al-
ready eros. While she prayed to and spoke with her
ally Afroditi, she largely ignored the mischievous
winged god who was to turn into Roman Cupid
and, for later painters with Christian themes, a cir-
cling chubby cherub. 38, 44a, 54, 130.

Gello A ghost of a girl who died young and haunted little children in Lesbos. Apparently it is a term for children who die young, for unknown reasons, and haunt other children. 178.

Geraistion A temple of Poseidon in Euboia. 96 (lines 21–37).

Gongyla One of Sappho's intimate friends. 22, 95.

Gorgo A rival of Sappho's; perhaps also a poet. 144.

Graces (Harites) The three Graces were daughters of Zeus and Eurynomi, but are also said to have been daughters of Dionysos and Afroditi. Their names were Algaia, Eufrosyni, and Thalia. They were the personifications of grace and beauty. They were friends of the Muses, with whom they lived on Olympos. Their favored art was poetry—hence they were the poet's muse. 53, 103, 128.

Gyrinno, Gyrinna One of Sappho's companions. In the poetic fragments she is Gyrinno, but she is Gyrinna in Maximus of Tyre's *Dissertations* 24.18.9, a commentary on homosexual love, which he compares to the Socratic art of love. 82a.

Hades Hades refers both to the god and to his underground hell, a gloomy and unseen abyss of the dead ruled by Hades himself and Persefoni (Persephone). Hades was separated from the upper earth by the rivers Styx (hate), Lethe (oblivion), Aheron (sorrow), Flegethon (fire), and Kokytos (wailing). Hades was also said to be located in the far west beyond human habitation, possibly the vast unknown extending through the Atlantic Ocean. The god Hades is Pluto in Latin.

In the war with Hades's Titan father, Kronos, the Titanomachy (war of the titans), three of his sons, Zeus, Poseidon, and Hades, won. They confined Kronos to dark Tartaros (an earthly hell); Zeus took possession of the sky, Poseidon the sea, and Hades the underworld. Hades was visited by the famous, among whom were Orfeus, Theseus, Achilles, Odysseus, and Aeneas. By trickery he abducted Persefoni and made her his wife for six months a year. 55.

Haraxos (Charaxos) Sappho's brother. 3, 5.

Hektor (Hector) Son of Priamos (Priam), husband of Andromache, and hero of the defense of Troy. Hektor was fated to die after he had killed Patroklas, Achilles's closest friend and lover. Raging with anger and vengeance, Achilles dragged Hektor's corpse three times around the walls of Troy to humiliate the hero's name. Hektor's funeral, portraying the grieving Andromache, is the last moving scene in the *Iliad*. 44.

Helen (Eléna) Daughter of Zeus and Lida (Leda), of extraordinary beauty. As the wife of Menelaos, she was seduced and abducted by Paris to Troy and so became the overt cause of the Trojan War. But Helen as a personage and symbol of beauty and candid passion was much greater than the capsule tale of Paris's girlfriend who irresponsibly skipped off to Ilios (Ilium) and caused a ten-year war. The strongest of the counters to the story about Helen's venture to Troy is found in a poem by the great Sicilian poet Stisihoros (Stesichorus), who cynically states about the whole "white-horsed myth" in his mocking poem "Recantation to Helen": "I spoke nonsense and I begin again: / The story is not true. / You never sailed on a benched ship. / You never entered the city of Troy."* Plato, in the *Phaidros,* picks up on "the false accusation of Helen," giving the background of Stisihoros's recantation: "When Stisihoros was blinded for having slandered Helen, he, unlike Homer, who was blinded for the same sin, wrote a palinode, a recantation, and immediately recovered his sight."

Of the many approaches, Sappho's is the most striking and convincing. She goes along with the Homeric legend but draws a different moral, making the power of love supreme. Yes, Helen left her worthy, dull, appointed husband, Menelaos, for the young Paris, but in her poem about her missing lover Anaktoria (16), who has also gone off to Sardis in the East, she cites Helen's escape to prove the ultimate worth of love, to which all may be sac-

* Willis Barnstone, trans., *Sappho and the Greek Lyric Poets* (New York: Schocken Books, 1987), p. 110.

rificed, including patriarchal conventions, family, and name. 16, 23.

Hera Queen of the Olympian gods, daughter of Kronos and Rhea, and mother of Hefaistos and Aris. In Rome she was Juno. Hera was the patron goddess of marriage and childbirth, and, beginning at Minoan Kriti, she was worshipped in all ancient periods throughout Greece, and many temples were built to adore her. Her husband and brother was Zeus.

Despite Hera's notoriety for being a plague to the cheating Zeus, Hera was also a protector of women and a powerful divinity. Sappho saw her in this latter light. Hera appears as a goddess to whom one makes a pilgrimage. There is no hint of the abused and vengeful deity. Rather, she is the closest equivalent to Sappho's ally Afroditi; Sappho describes her as beautiful and dazzling, and she prays to her for help. *See* Artemis, *and also* Aris, Dionysos, *and* Zeus. 9, 17.

Hermioni (Hermione) The only daughter of Menelaos and Helen. Her beauty did not match the beauty of her mother, Helen. When Helen eloped with Paris, Hermioni was left to be brought up by Agamemnon's wife, Klytemnestra. 23.

Hermis (Hermes) Athletic son of Zeus and Maia, he was the cupbearer and messenger of the gods and a psychopomp, that is, a guide of the dead to Hades. He was also the god of commerce, travelers, good luck, poets, and thieves and an extraordinary inventor credited with having invented music, the shepherd's lyre (made of cow intestines and tortoise shell), the flute, numbers, the alphabet, and gymnastics. As a messenger, he was represented with a winged hat, winged sandals, and a caduceus, a winged staff with two snakes twined around it that has become the emblematic staff of the medical profession. He was also a god of fertility and sexuality. His monument was usually the *herma,* a stone pillar with a head on top and a phallus in the center that was found outside houses as a good-luck symbol. Religious figures were named for him, most notably Hermis Trismegistos (thrice-strong Hermis), and there was the hermetic tradition in philosophy and magic. In literary criticism, we have hermeneutics, which is a method and theory of textual interpretation. Hermis was also a fun god, a humorous messenger often into mischief. He had three sons, of whom the best known was the satyr Pan, an amusing god of the woods and flocks, with a human torso and goat's legs and horns, whom Picasso resurrected with sensuality and glee. With Afroditi, Hermis fathered Hermafroditos, who became a hermaphrodite. In Rome Hermis was the popular Mercury. 141a, b.

Hesperos The evening star, son of Astraios or Kephalos or Atlas and Eos (Dawn), and father of the Hesperides.

Hesperos is also the planet Venus (Afroditi). 104a, 104b.

Hymen (Hymenaios) God of marriage, a handsome youth whom it was customary to invoke at Greek weddings by singing "Hymen, O Hymen," in the hymneal or bridal song. 111.

Idaos The herald or messenger, who is probably from Ida, a mountain area near Troy. In the *Iliad,* he appears as the chief herald of Troy. 44.

Ilion (Ilium, Ilum) is the city of Troy (Troía), now called Hissarlik in Turkish. Homer's *Iliad* deals with the siege of Troy. It is not known whether the present site, the nine walls identified and excavated by Heinrich Schliemann in 1871, is actually Troy, where and whether the Trojan War actually took place, or whether Homer made a supreme amalgam of Bronze Age stories. There is no defining archeological or textual evidence of the events of the war. Near the Schliemann site is a Phrygian city called Troy, in a region known as the Troas or the Troad. 44.

Ilos Father of Priamos (Priam) and founder of Troy. 44.

Ionian Referring to Greeks in an area of the west coast of Asia Minor. 98a.

Irana (Oirana) One of Sappho's friends. Irana can be a friend's name or mean "peace." Its usage here is ambiguous. 91, 135.

Jason Leader of the Argonauts, who set sail in the *Argo* to find the Golden Fleece, which he hoped to bring to his uncle Pelias in exchange for his patrimony. He obtained the fleece with the help of Medea, whom he later married. 152.

Kastor (Castor) One of the Dioskouroi. *See* Dioskouroi. 166.

Kleanaktidai The children of Kleanax, including his son Myrsilos; they were a ruling family during Sappho's life. 98b.

Kleis Name of Sappho's daughter, also her mother, and perhaps a friend. 98b, 132.

Knossos Ancient capital of the Minoan kingdom and site of the palace of Minos, which has been associated with the labyrinth and the Minotaur (the bull of Minos). 2.

Koios (Coeus) A Titan, mother of Lito and hence grandmother of Apollo and Artemis. 44a.

Kriti The island of Crete. 2.

Kydro A friend of Sappho's. 19.

Kypris (Cyprus) One of the names of Afroditi, meaning she is a Kyprian (Cypriote).

Kypros The large Greek island of Kypros (Cyprus), near the coast of Syria, was one of the chief seats of worship of Afroditi.

Kypros-born (Cyprus-born) Another name for Afroditi. *See also* Afroditi.

Kythereia (Kytherea, Cytherea) A surname of Afroditi, meaning one who comes from Kythera. Kythera was a city in Kriti (Crete). Kythera was also the name of one of the seven Ionian islands off the eastern coast of the Peloponnisos. Both the Kritan city of Kythera and the Ionian island of Kythera are associated with a seat for worshiping Afroditi. There was also a tradition that Afroditi rose from the sea near Kythera. *See also* Afroditi. 86, 140.

Lesbian See Lesbos.

Lesbos The ancient name of the island of Mytilini, whose modern name comes from that of its main city in antiquity. The dialect of Lesbos was Aiolic, in which Sappho and Alkaios wrote. The name Lesbos is still used in speech, and also on maps, though usually in parenthesis. Lowercase "lesbian" refers to a woman whose sexual orientation is to women. 106.

Lida (Leda) Mother of Helen, the Dioskouroi, and in some versions Klytemnestra, and wife of Tyndareus. She was seduced by Zeus, who came to her, as readers of Yeats know, in the form of a swan. Another version, to which Sappho alludes, has Nemesis lay an egg, which Lida found and cared for and from which came Helen. 166.

Megara A friend of Sappho. 68a.

Mika Probably a shortened form of Mnasidika. Mika was a companion or a rival who had gone over to the house of Penthilos, a clan who were the ruling nobles of Mytilini. Sappho's family opposed the Penthelids, who had probably forced Sappho and her family to go into exile. 71.

Mnasidika A friend of Sappho's who appears to have deserted her. *See also* Mika. 82a.

Muses (Mousai) Daughters of Zeus and Mnemosyni (Memory), the nine muses lived on Mount Helikon, where they presided over the arts and sciences. They were worshipped early on in mountainous Pieria in Thessaly. Therefore, they were often called the Pierides. The muses were also worshipped on Mount Parnassos, and at Delfi, where Apollo was said to be their leader. 58, 103, 127, 128, 150.

Myrsilos Tyrant of Mytilini who probably caused the exile of Alkaios and Sappho.

Mytilini (Mitylene) Ancient and modern capital of Lesbos, or Mytilini, where Sappho spent much of her life. The dialect of Lesbos was Aiolic, in which Sappho and Alkaios wrote.

Nereids Sea nymphs, fifty daughters of Nereus. 5.

Nereus Son of Pontos, husband of the Oceanid Doris, and father of the Nereids, Nereus was the wise "old man of the sea." The Nereids often accompanied Poseidon and helped sailors in time of storm in the Mediterranean.

Niobi (Niobe) Daughter of Tantalos and wife of Amfion, Niobi boasted to Lito that her family was larger than Lito's, and to avenge this insult Lito's children, Apollo and Artemis, killed the twelve to twenty children of Niobi. 142.

Olympos (Olympus) Home of the Greek gods and the highest mountain in Greece. The Olympic Games were held every four years on the plains below the mountain in honor of Zeus. They included not only athletic events but contests of choral poetry and dance, and at times drama, which included choral dance. An Olympian was a Greek god or goddess. 27.

Paean Epithet of Apollo. 44.

Pafian Of Pafos (Paphos), and therefore Afroditi. *See also* Afroditi.

Pandion King of Athens whose daughters Filomela and Prokni were turned into a swallow and a nightingale, respectively (Latin tradition reversed the order). The presence of a swallow often portended a forthcoming event. 135.

Peitho The personification of persuasion, and the daughter or attendant of Afroditi. 96 (lines 21–37).

Penthilos A rival family of ruling nobles in Mytilini. *See also* Mika, Mnasidika. 71.

Persefoni (Persephone) Daughter of Dimitir and Zeus, she was a goddess of fertility and vegetation and the unwilling queen of the underworld. In Sicily she was abducted by Hades and taken to the underworld, where he held her captive in his darknesses. Persefoni spent the winter in Hades and rose to the earth in the spring. She had a slight graveyard smell when she arrived, it was said, but she soon became flowery. Her return to the underworld signified the withering of flowers and grain.

The Eleusinian mysteries celebrated Persefoni's cycle of birth, death, and rebirth, in which she appeared under the name of Kore (a virgin). In Rome Persefoni was Proserpina or Proserpine. *See also* Afroditi, Dionysos. 158 Diehl.

Persuasion See Peitho.

Phoebus (Foibus) An epithet of Apollo, meaning "shining." 44a.

Phokaia A city of Ionia in Asia Minor, southeast of Mytilini. 101.

Pierian Of Pieria, a region of Thrace in Macedonia, where the Muses were first worshipped. 103.

Pittakos Tyrant, statesman, and sage of Lesbos in Sappho's time, depending on the view of the inhabitant; married the sister of Drakon; former ruler who was the son of Penthilos. Pittakos was initially an ally of both Alkaios's and Sappho's families, but later he joined with the party of another ruler, Myrsilos, an enemy of both Sappho and Alkaios. *See also* Myrsilos.

Pleiades Seven daughters of Atlas and virgin companions of Artemis. When pursued by the giant hunter Orion, their prayers were answered when they were changed into doves (*pleiades*) and placed among the stars. Their names were Maia, Meropi,

Elektra, Kelaino, Taygeti, Sterop (or Asteropi), and Alkyoni. 168b.

Polyanax Father of Polyanaktidis and member of the important Polyanaktid family in Lesbos. 155.

Polydeukis (Pollux) One of the Dioskouroi. *See* Dioskouroi. 166.

Priamos (Priam) King of Troy during the Trojan War, he was the father of twenty children by Hecuba, including Hektor, Paris, and Kassandra. When his son Hektor was killed, he went into the Greek (Achaean) camp and begged Achilles for the body so he could be properly buried. Achilles agreed to the request. *See also* Hektor. 44.

Psapfo (Sappho) Born about 612 B.C.E. in either Eressos or Mytilini on the island of Lesbos, Sappho wrote lyric poems in her own Aiolic dialect, in which she referred to herself as Psapfo. 1; 65; 94; 133a, b.

Sappho See Psapfo.

Sardis Ancient city of Asia Minor and capital of the kingdom of Lydia. 96, 98a.

Semili (Semele) *See* Thyoni *and* Dionysos.

Thebe, Thebes Not the more famous cities in Boitia and Egypt but a holy city near Mount Ida in the Troad in which Andromache's father, Etion, was both king and high priest.

Thyoni (Thyone), also known as Semili (Semele). Thyoni was the daughter of Kadmos and Zeus, and the mother of Dionysos. 17.

Tithonos Brother of Priamos and lover of Eos (Dawn), who left him each morning. Through the prayers of Eos, he became immortal, but he did not retain his youth and so became synonymous with a decrepit old man. 58.

Tros The mythical founder of Troy.

Tyndareus A king of Sparta and Lida's husband; he fathered Helen, Klytemnestra, and the Dioskouroi, though most legends see him as a cuckold, with Zeus being the actual father of Helen and also of Polydeukis (Pollux).

Zeus or Dias Son of Kronos and Rhea, brother of Poseidon, Hades, Hestia, Dimitir, and Hera, who was also his wife, Zeus was the supreme Olympic god. He determined good and evil as judge, and he carried the thunderbolt as his weapon of choice, though he had many powers of life, death, and transformation at his disposal. He was the archetypal Greek deity. At the same time, he was almost helplessly or whimsically human, resorting to all manner of disguises and metamorphoses to deceive his sister-wife Hera and conceal romances with other goddesses and mortals. 1, 17, 53, 96, 102.

BIBLIOGRAPHY

Editions, Studies, and Translations

Abbott, Sidney, and Barbara Love. *Sappho Was a Right-On Woman: A Liberated View of Lesbianism.* 1972. Reprint, New York: Stein and Day, 1985.

Balmer, Josephine. *Sappho: Poems and Fragments.* New York: Meadowland Books, 1993.

Barnard, Mary, trans. *Sappho.* Berkeley: University of California Press, 1958.

Barnstone, Willis. *The Poetics of Ecstasy: From Sappho to Borges.* New York: Holmes and Meier, 1983.

_____. *The Poetics of Translation: History, Theory, Practice.* New Haven: Yale University Press, 1993.

_____, trans. *Sappho and the Greek Lyric Poets.* Introduction by William E. McCulloh. New York: Schocken Books, 1987.

_____. *Sappho: Lyrics in the Original Greek with Translations.* Preface by A. R. Burn. New York: New York University Press, 1965. First published 1965 by Doubleday Anchor Books.

_____. *Sappho, Poems: A New Version.* Los Angeles: Sun and Moon Press, 1998.

Beaumont, Edith de, trans. *Poèmes de Sappho.* Illustrations by Marie Laurencin. One copy in the Kinsey Institute, Indiana University, Bloomington.

Bergk, T. *Poetae Lyrici Graeci.* 3 vols. Leipzig: B. G. Teubner, 1882.

Boardman, John, and E. La Rocca. *Eros in Greece.* London: Phaidon, 1978.

Bonnard, Andre, ed. and trans. *Poésies de Sappho.* Illustrations by Rodin. Lausanne: Mermod, 1948.

Bowie, A. M. *The Poetic Dialect of Sappho and Alcaeus.* New York: Arno Press, 1981.

Bowra, Cecil Maurice. *Greek Lyric Poetry: From Alman to Simonides.* 2nd rev. ed. Oxford: Oxford University Press, 1961.

Bremmer, Jan., ed. *From Sappho to de Sade*: *Moments in the History of Sexuality.* London: Routledge, 1989.

Burn, A. R. *The Lyric Age of Greece.* London: Edward Arnold, 1978.

Burnett, Anne Pippin. *Three Archaic Poets: Archilochus, Alcaeus, Sappho.* Cambridge, Mass.: Harvard University Press, 1983.

Campbell, David A. *The Golden Lyre: The Themes of the Greek Lyric Poets.* London: Duckworth, 1983.

———, ed. *Greek Lyric Poetry: A Selection.* London: Macmillan, 1967.

———, ed. and trans. *Sappho and Alcaeus.* Vol. 1 of *Greek Lyric.* Loeb Classical Library. Cambridge, Mass.: Harvard University Press, 1988.

Carson, Anne. *Eros the Bittersweet*. Princeton, N.J.: Princeton University Press, 1986.

———, trans. *If Not, Winter: Fragments of Sappho*. New York: Vintage Books, 2002.

Chandler, Robert, ed. and trans. *Sappho*. Introduction by Richard Jenkyns. London: J. M. Dent, 1998.

Davenport, Guy, trans. *Archilochos, Sappho, Alkman: Three Lyric Poets of the Late Greek Bronze Age*. Berkeley: University of California Press, 1980.

———, trans. *Poems and Fragments*. Ann Arbor: University of Michigan Press, 1965.

———, trans. *Seven Greeks*. New York: New Directions, 1995.

Davison, J. A. *From Archilochus to Pindar*. London: Macmillan, 1968.

Diehl, Ernest. *Anthologia Lyrica Graeca*. Vol. 1. Leipzig: B. G. Teubner, 1964.

Dover, K. J. *Greek Homosexuality*. London: Duckworth, 1978.

Duban, Jeffrey M. *Ancient and Modern Images of Sappho: Translations and Studies in Archaic Greek Love Lyric*. Lanham, Md.: University Press of America, 1983.

DuBois, Page. *Sappho Is Burning*. Chicago: University of Chicago Press, 1995.

Edmonds, J. M., ed. and trans. *Lyra Graeca*. Vol. 1. 2nd printing. London: William Heinemann, 1928.

Fränkel, Hermann. *Early Greek Poetry and Philosophy*.

Translated by Moses Hadas and James Willis. New York: Harcourt Brace Jovanovich, 1962.

Freedman, Nancy Mars. *Sappho: The Tenth Muse.* New York: St. Martin's Press, 1998.

Gentili, Bruno. *Poetry and Its Public in Ancient Greece.* Translated by A. Thomas Cole. Baltimore: Johns Hopkins University Press, 1988.

Gerber, D. E. *Euterpe: An Anthology of Early Greek Lyric, Elegiac and Iambic Poetry.* Amsterdam: Hakkert, 1970.

Grahn, Judy. *The Highest Apple: Sappho and the Lesbian Poetic Tradition.* San Francisco: Spinsters Ink, 1985.

Greek Anthology. Edited by W. R. Paton. 5 vols. Cambridge, Mass.: Harvard University Press, 1916–1918.

Green, Ellen, ed. *Reading Sappho: Reception and Transmission.* Berkeley: University of California Press, 1996.

_____, ed. *Re-Reading Sappho: Reception and Transmission.* Berkeley: University of California Press, 1996.

H.D. (Hilda Doolittle). *Notes on Thought and Vision, and The Wise Sappho.* London: Peter Owen, 1988.

Hutchinson, G. O. *Greek Lyric Poetry: A Commentary on Selected Larger Pieces: Alcman, Stesichorus, Sappho, Alceaus, Ibycus, Anacreon, Simonides, Bacchylides, Pindar, Sophocles, Euripides.* Oxford: Oxford University Press, 2001.

Jay, Peter, and Caroline Lewis, eds. *Sappho through English Poetry.* London: Anvil Press Poetry, 1996.

Jenkyns, R. *Three Classical Poets: Sappho, Catullus, Juvenal.* Cambridge, Mass.: Harvard University Press, 1982.

Kirkwood, Gordon M. *Early Greek Monody.* Cornell Studies in Classical Philology 37. Ithaca, N.Y.: Cornell University Press, 1974.

Lattimore, Richmond, trans. "Sappho: Selections." In *Greek Lyrics.* 2nd ed. Chicago: University of Chicago Press, 1960.

Ledwidge, Bernard. *Sappho: La première voix d'une femme.* Paris: Mercure de France, 1987.

Lefkowitz, Mary R. *Heroines and Hysterics.* London: Duckworth, 1981.

Lobel, Edgar, and Denys Page, eds. *Poetarum Lesbiorum Fragmenta.* Oxford: Oxford University Press, 1955.

Lombardo, Stanley. *Poems and Fragments.* Edited by Susan Warden; introduction by Pamela Gordon. Indianapolis: Hackett, 2002.

Longinus. *Longinus on Sublimity.* Translated by D. A. Russell. Oxford: Oxford University Press, 1966.

———. *On the Sublime.* Edited by D. A. Russell. Oxford: Oxford University Press, 1964.

Marx, Olga, and Ernst Morwitz, trans. *Poems of Alcman, Sappho, Ibycus.* New York: Alfred A. Knopf, 1945.

Nims, John Frederick. *Sappho to Valéry: Poems in Translation.* New Brunswick, N.J.: Rutgers University Press, 1971.

Page, Denys. *Epigrammata Graeca*. Oxford: Oxford University Press, 1975.

▬▬▬▬. *Poetae Melici Graeci*. Oxford: Oxford University Press, 1962.

▬▬▬▬. *Sappho and Alcaeus: An Introduction to the Study of Ancient Lesbian Poetry*. Oxford: Clarendon Press, 1979.

▬▬▬▬. *Sappho and Alcaeus*. Oxford: Oxford University Press, 1959.

Picasso, Pablo. *Grâce et mouvement: 14 compositions originales, gravées sur cuivre*. Edited by Louis Grosclaude. Issued in portfolio. "Sappho, 14 poèmes," pp. 17–32. Zurich: Presses des Conzett and Huber, 1943.

Pomeroy, Sarah. *Goddesses, Whores, Wives, and Slaves: Women in Classical Antiquity*. New York: Schocken Books, 1975.

Pope, Alexander. *The Works of Alexander Pope Esq.* Vol. 3, *Consisting of Fables, Translations, and Imitations*. London: printed for H. Lintot, 1736.

Powell, Jim, trans. *Sappho, a Garland: The Poems and Fragments*. New York: Farrar, Straus, Giroux, 1993.

Prins, Yopie. *Victorian Sappho*. Princeton, N.J.: Princeton University Press, 1999.

Quasimodo, Salvatore. *Lirici greci*. Translated by Luciano Anceschi. Milan: A. Mondadori, 1960.

Rabinowitz, Nancy Sorkin. *Among Women: From the Homosocial to the Homoerotic in the Ancient World*. Austin: University of Texas Press, 2002.

Rayor, Diane J., trans. *Sappho Poems*. With illustrations by Janet Steinmetz. Colorado Springs: Press at Colorado College, 1980.

Reynolds, Margaret. *History of Sappho*. New York: Vintage Books, 1999.

———. *The Sappho History*. New York: Palgrave Macmillan, 2003.

Rissman, Leah. *Love as War: Homeric Allusion in the Poetry of Sappho*. Konigstein, Germany: Hain, 1983.

Robinson, David Moore. *Sappho and Her Influence*. New York: Cooper Square Publishers, 1963.

Roche, Paul, trans. *The Love Songs of Sappho*. Introduction by Page Dubois. New York: Signet Classic, 1991.

Rosenmeyer, Thomas G., James W. Halporn, and Martin Ostwald. *The Meters of Greek and Latin Poetry*. New York: Bobbs-Merrill, 1963.

Segal, Charles. *Aglaia: The Poetry of Alcman, Sappho, Pindar, Bacchylides, and Corinna*. Lanham, Md.: Rowman & Littlefield, 1998.

Snyder, Jane McIntosh. *Lesbian Desire in the Lyrics of Sappho*. New York: Columbia University Press, 1997.

Treu, Max, ed. and trans. *Sappho*. Munich: Ernst Heimeran Verlag, 1963.

Voigt, Eva-Maria, ed. *Sappho et Alcaeus: Fragmenta*. Amsterdam: Athenaeum, 1971.

West, M. L. *Greek Metre*. New York: Oxford University Press, 1982.

Wilamowitz-Moellendorff, Ulrich von. *Sappho und Simonides*. Berlin: Weidmann, 1966.

Wilhelm, James J. *Gay and Lesbian Poetry: An Anthology from Sappho to Michelangelo*. New York: Garland, 1995.

Wilson, Lyn Hatherly. *Sappho's Sweetbitter Songs: Configurations of Female and Male in Ancient Greek Lyric*. New York: Routledge, 1996.

SHAMBHALA POCKET LIBRARY

Mindfulness on the Go
Jan Chozen Bays

Narrow Road to the Interior:
and Other Writings
Matsuo Bashō; translated by Sam Hamill

The Path of Insight Meditation
Jack Kornfield and Joseph Goldstein

The Pocket Chögyam Trungpa
Compiled and edited by Carolyn Rose Gimian

The Pocket Dalai Lama
Edited by Mary Craig

The Pocket Meister Eckhart
Edited by David O'Neal

The Pocket Pema Chödrön
Edited by Eden Steinberg

The Pocket Rumi
Edited by Kabir Helminski

The Pocket Sappho
Translated by Willis Barnstone

Pocket Taoist Wisdom
Translated and edited by Thomas Cleary

The Pocket Thich Nhat Hanh
Compiled and edited by Melvin McLeod

The Pocket Thomas Merton
Edited by Robert Inchausti

Shambhala: The Sacred Path of the Warrior
Chögyam Trungpa

Siddhartha
Hermann Hesse; translated by Sherab Chödzin Kohn

Song of Myself
Walt Whitman; edited by Stephen Mitchell

The Spiritual Teaching of Ramana Maharshi
Ramana Maharshi

The Spring of My Life: and Selected Haiku
Kobayashi Issa; translated by Sam Hamill

Tao Teh Ching
Lao Tzu; translated by John C. H. Wu

Teachings of the Christian Mystics
Edited by Andrew Harvey

Teachings of the Hindu Mystics
Edited by Andrew Harvey

The Tibetan Book of the Dead
Translated by Francesca Fremantle and Chögyam Trungpa

Walden: Selections from the American Classic
Henry David Thoreau

The Wisdom of the Buddha
Compiled and edited by Anne Bancroft

The Wisdom of Tibetan Buddhism
Edited by Reginald A. Ray